How

MAINE

Changed the

WORLD

Down East Books

An imprint of The Globe Pequot Publishing Group, Inc.
64 South Main Street
Essex, CT 06426
www.globepequot.com

Distributed by NATIONAL BOOK NETWORK

Photographs: Dennis Jarvis,6; Dan Tobyne,8,86; Billy Hathorn,10,114; iStock487856433:e-doma,11; iStock144321095:futureimage,14; Acroterion,17; Thomas MacMillan,20; Seeds of Peace,21; iStock466981087:PetrMalyshev,22; MagicPiano,23,57; Cliff1066,26; Holt Co.,26; Stanley Museum,27,28; iStock500599289:MikeMcKinne,30; iStock500874254:E.J.JohnsonPhotography,31; iStock500955872:E.J.JohnsonPhotography,32; iStock627202312:SeanPavonePhoto,34; A.B.K.Fenris, 36; iStock488651559:AnnaAndich, 38; iStock152946126:MikeDoc1968,41; Julia Ess,50; AuroraPhotos|AlamyStockPhotoCRG8X8,51; iStock185126468:JonathanSloane,65; Benjamin B. Hampton, Peary-MacMillan Arctic Museum,67; McDougall&Keefe, Library of Congress,67; Margaret Chase Smith Library,69,71; iStock614303646:G.Sheldon,77; iStock177558720:erineb745,78; JRC903,85; Goyk,87; PAImages|AlamyStockPhotosG9XC7F,89; iStock681899842:Krugloff,95; Cary5750,105; Collections of Aroostook County Historical and Art Museum,109; iStock176957097:Gino'sPhotos,118; Smallbones,125; Erasergirl,126; RIANovosti,131; Allen Warren,132

Designed by Lynda Chilton, Chilton Creative

British Library Cataloguing in Publication Information available

Library of Congress Cataloging-in-Publication Data available

ISBN 978-1-60893-631-1 (hardcover)
ISBN 978-1-60893-632-8 (e-book)

How

MAINE

Changed the

WORLD

A HISTORY IN 50 PEOPLE, PLACES, AND OBJECTS

NANCY GRIFFIN

Down East Books

CONTENTS

A 31-foot statue of Paul Bunyan stands on Bangor's Main Street. Some say he's mythical, but Mainers say he's from Bangor. In his hand, this giant lumberjack holds the tool of his trade. You guessed it—a peavey.

The Peavey

LOGGING AND FOREST PRODUCTS HAVE TRADITIONALLY BEEN AMONG MAINE'S biggest industries, starting in the 17th century when Maine pines supplied ship masts for the British Navy. The state's first sawmill was built in 1634 and in the 1800s Bangor was the "Lumber Capital of the World." Later, masts and lumber gave way to pulp and paper, and though today the industry is in decline, forest products still contribute around $8.5 billion annually to Maine's economy.

For a couple of centuries, logging was done in pretty much the same way. Trees were felled by hand and logs were hauled to the river and floated to the nearest sawmill. Logjams in the river were cleared by hand. Every aspect of logging was physically demanding and extremely dangerous.

In 1857 blacksmith Joseph Peavey was watching loggers trying to clear a jam on the Stillwater branch of the Penobscot River, a primary logging river in the state. He quickly realized they needed a better tool for the task.

He returned to his shop and came up with the idea for a clasp, connected by a bolt on which to hang a hook, with a sharp pick on the end of a long stick. This was a modification and improvement to the existing cant dog—which had a blunt tip—that lumbermen had used for years.

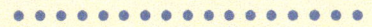

No stranger to invention, Peavey is also credited with inventing the first hay press, the first clapboard water steel, a spill-proof inkwell, and a hoist for pulling stumps and lifting dam gates.

The peavey caught on immediately and it's still in use even though log drives down the river were banned in 1976. The tool is used by loggers at mills, in the woods, anyplace where they still wrangle logs around, dislodge rocks, tighten chains, or dislodge trees—the peavey really is an all-purpose tool.

Peavey made the tool in his blacksmith shop until the demand grew too great. Over the years, he moved the manufacturing around, but eventually the Peavey Manufacturing Company was built just five miles down the river from the place of his original inspiration. The company has made the peavey continuously since 1857 and still ships them wherever they are needed.

On August 31, 1899, the Stanley-designed Locomobile, driven by F. O. Stanley, set another record. With his wife, Flora, F.O. drove to the top of Mt. Washington in New Hampshire. Tackling the rocky carriage road, they made it to the top in two hours and ten minutes, the first car to drive all the way up the 6,288-foot mountain.

Stanley Steamer

IN 1896, AUTOMOBILES WERE RARE AND FEW MODELS OF THE EXPERIMENTAL horseless carriages could be found. When an exhibition was announced for Brockton, Massachusetts, inventive twin brothers Francis Edgar and Freelan Oscar Stanley from Kingfield, Maine, decided to attend. They watched a French import, billed as "The Marvel of the Age," limp and puff around a half-mile track, jerking and stalling all the while.

On the train ride home, the brothers were asked if they would buy one of the horseless carriages. F.E. replied, "No. But I'm going to make a better one."

A year later, F.E. unveiled his prototype, and by 1898 the brothers had produced three more cars. In 1899, they brought their car to New England's first motor show in Boston. Competing against an electric car, a gasoline-powered car, and another steam car, the Stanley Steamer beat the others, completing three laps of a one-third-mile track in two minutes eleven seconds—a world record. The Stanley was also the only car to make it to the top of the slight incline set up for the competition.

The fame from the win resulted in 200 orders for cars and launched the Stanley Motor Carriage Company. The brothers bought an old factory in Newton, Massachusetts, and set up the first automobile assembly line in the world. In March 1899, before they'd even completed their first prototype, the owner of *Cosmopolitan* magazine, John Brisbane Walker, offered to buy

At "Speed Week" in 1906, the Stanley brothers' red racer, known as the "Wogglebug," shattered the world speed record by 18 miles for a run of 127.66 mph, the first time an automobile had traveled faster than two miles a minute. Later that week, the driver tried to beat his own record. He was traveling at 150 mph when he hit a rough spot in the sand and rolled into the surf. Although he recovered, the Stanleys never raced their cars again. The record was not beaten until 1910, and was never beaten in the same weight class.

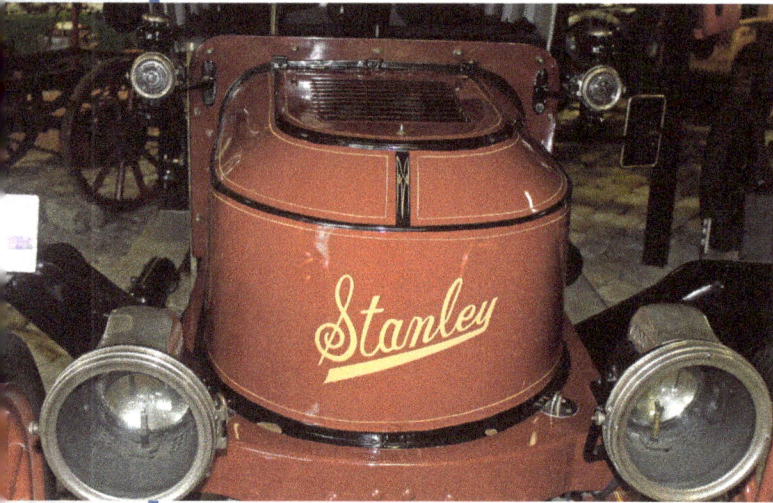
This Stanley is on display at the Cole Land Transportation Museum in Bangor, Maine.a

half-interest in their company. The twins turned him down. A month later, with production in full swing, Walker came back with another offer, this time to buy the entire company.

F.E. and F.O. had no intention of selling, but they had promised to give the tycoon a price, so they chose an astronomical figure: $250,000. To their shock, Walker agreed and the sale was made. Walker enlisted "The Asphalt King," Amzi Lorenzo Barber, as a full partner and they renamed the company the Locomobile Company.

The Stanleys sold all their designs and patents and agreed not to build a steam car for a year. Walker and Barber, however, had a falling out and split into two companies: Locomobile and Mobile. Each hired a Stanley brother as a consultant, so the twins helped build cars they had designed for competing companies they didn't own.

Within a year, the Locomobile Company stopped production and the twins were able to buy back their patents, designs, and an improved factory for 10 percent of the sale price.

As the brothers improved their designs, making the cars faster and sleeker, they entered the steamers in races. In January 1906, their friend and head of their repair shop, Fred H. Marriott, raced the Stanley Rocket racer at the Ormond Beach, Florida, "Speed Week." Marriott raced against the best cars from Europe and the U.S., including Lancia, Fiat, and Mercedes. He beat all entries in a one-mile race, then won a thirty-mile race by a wide margin. In the week's last event, he drove around for several miles, getting up speed before he hit the measured mile in the world speed record event.

In 1917, the Stanley twins retired from the steamer business, turning the company over to their sons-in-law. Manufactured from 1896 to 1924, the Stanley Steamer was the best-known and best-selling steam car of all time.

Machine Gun

3

HIRAM STEVENS MAXIM BEGAN WORKING AT AGE FOURTEEN. BORN IN THE SMALL TOWN of Sangerville, Maine, on February 5, 1840, he displayed an inventive bent from an early age. His first patent, for a hair-curling iron, was granted in 1866. Soon after, he patented a device for generating illuminating gas, then a locomotive headlight—those were the first of the 271 patents (122 in the Unied States, 149 in England) he would accrue in his lifetime.

By 1878, he was hired as chief engineer for the United States Electric Lighting Company, the nation's first such company. Maxim invented a method of manufacturing carbon filaments for light bulbs. He was the first to install electric lights in a New York City building. Maxim was also embroiled in several patent disputes with Thomas Edison, claiming that, in fact, he had invented the light bulb.

After demonstrating his electric pressure regulator at the Paris Exhibition in 1881, he was awarded France's prestigious Legion d'Honneur. That same year he moved to England and began work on his machine gun. Accounts say that as a child Maxim had been knocked over by a rifle's recoil and the experience inspired him to try to find a way to use the recoil force to operate a gun automatically. And Maxim had supposedly encountered an American in Vienna who encouraged him to stop working on electricity, saying that if he wanted to make a pile of money, he should:

King Edward VII of England firing a Maxim gun, c. 1901

" . . .invent something that will enable these Europeans to cut each other's throats with greater facility."

11

From 1883 through 1885 Maxim patented several methods of automatic operation, including gas and blowback. The Gatling machine gun already existed, but it was powered by a hand crank. Its rotating barrels achieved a maximum firing rate of 1,200 rounds per minute. When Maxim finally harnessed the recoil power of each bullet to eject the spent cartridge and draw in the next, his portable machine gun needed only one barrel to fire all its bullets automatically, simply by holding the trigger.

In 1884, he founded the Maxim Gun Company in England and later licensed his gun for use by the British Army. Five other countries—Germany, Austria, Italy, Switzerland, and Russia—installed the gun in their armories a year later. Maxim became an English citizen in 1900 and was knighted a year later.

Hiram wasn't the only inventor in the family. His brother Hudson was a military inventor specializing in explosives. Hudson went to England to work on a smokeless powder with his brother, and one of them invented cordite—though it isn't clear which one of them. The patent was issued simply to H. Maxim, and it is generally believed that Hudson was the true inventor, but based on the ambiguity of that initial, Hiram placed a solo claim to it in England. Hudson returned to the States and claimed the patent here. The claims, counter claims, and court disputes left the brothers' relationship in shambles. But cordite greatly increased the effectiveness of the machine gun because the lack of smoke meant the enemy was unlikely to spot the machine gun's location.

Hiram Maxim will always be remembered first and perhaps only for the invention of the machine gun, but he made a contribution to health as well as death. A sufferer from chronic bronchitis for the last sixteen years of his life, he invented a menthol pocket inhaler and a larger inhaler that used menthol and evergreen mixed with water. The vapors produced from a heated glass bulb he called the "Pipe of Peace" could be inhaled directly to the back of the throat. He produced and sold several

THE MACHINE GUN WAR

Variations of Maxim's design were used by both sides during World War I. His weapon forever changed the face of war and the concept of trench warfare was developed as a way to counter its devastating effects. Maxim died on November 24, 1916, just days after the end of the Battle of the Somme. He missed perhaps the four bloodiest months of the war, in which more than one million people were killed.

This British Vickers machine gun is a Maxim design, made after Vickers acquired his company. The gun crew is wearing gas masks at the Battle of the Somme, July 1916.

hundred thousand of the devices. Despite some criticism of the devices, the inhaler may have kept him alive until age 76. He wrote in his 1915 autobiography:

> "It will be seen that it is a very creditable thing to invent
> a killing machine, and nothing less than a disgrace to invent
> an apparatus to prevent human suffering."

Maxim also experimented with flight, and while he failed to build a useful airplane, his steam-powered craft proved that flight could be achieved in a heavier-than-air device. Other inventions of his include: the first automated sprinkler system, devices to prevent the rolling of ships, mango-electric machines, variations on oil, steam, and gas engines; an aerial torpedo gun, eyelet and riveting machines, aircraft artillery, and coffee substitutes.

If his real flying machines amounted to little, in England he might also be remembered for his "Captive Flying Machine," an amusement ride found on many British fairgrounds. He based the ride on a test device he built for the Earl's Court exhibition of 1904, hoping to draw attention to actual flight. Cars hang captive from a spinning frame and rise as it spins. One of the originals is still in operation in Blackpool at Pleasure Beach amusement park.

4

Toothpick

MAINE DIDN'T INVENT THE TOOTHPICK–IT'S AN ANCIENT DEVICE–BUT A MAINE TOWN became the world center for toothpick manufacturing.

Most people have probably never given a second thought to the humble, tiny toothpick. But for many years, the residents of Strong cared very deeply about the toothpick.

This town of around 1,000 people once produced 95 percent of all toothpicks made in the United States. Determining the ideal wood for toothpicks was white birch, Bostonian Charles Forster established his Forster Manufacturing Company near the source and began mass producing toothpicks by the millions daily.

Output from Forster's factory peaked at 20 million toothpicks a day, making Strong the "Toothpick Capital of the World." When his patent expired in 1880, his plant had competition from factories in nearby towns, although there seemed to be room enough for everyone. Production in the U.S. reached more than 25 billion by 1910. And following the Depression and World War II, production soared to a peak of 75 billion toothpicks a year.

At one point, Forster refined the original flat design to a more comfortable, rounded product. By the 1990s, production slumped due to overseas manufacturers producing toothpicks more cheaply. Forster's went from selling toothpicks around the world to watching imported toothpicks diminish their business. The mill closed in 2003, marking the end of Maine-made toothpicks.

Charles Forster was working in Brazil, using a hand-whittled orangewood toothpick when the proverbial light bulb went off. He recognized that a gap existed between the artisan-made toothpick devices made for the wealthy and the offhand use of a twig or a thorn by the poor. Forster envisioned a mass-produced toothpick, affordable by all. He started by importing Brazilian toothpicks briefly but then bought the patent of Benjamin Franklin Sturtevant's machine that cut logs into thin strips for shoe pegs. He tinkered for years along with mechanic Charles Freeman to produce a proper veneer for stamping out toothpicks. Success arrived with a patent in 1860.

The Forster mill in Strong, ca 1940s.

Naturally, manufacturing a product in the remote Maine woods does not guarantee success, but Forster was also a marketing genius. Toothpicks had not been readily available to the masses, and tooth-picking in public was frowned upon in the U.S. So Forster hired Harvard students to request a toothpick after their meals at fancy Boston restaurants. When the students were informed that the restaurant had none, they were urged to complain loudly and announce they would never eat there again.

Forster also employed young men to stand outside those same fancy restaurants, picking their teeth with his toothpicks, which implied they had recently dined there. Toothpick use soared and the practice caught on, even among young ladies.

Finally, Forster employees were sent to retail shops to ask for wooden toothpicks. Soon after the shops admitted that they didn't carry toothpicks, Forster would show up to offer his product to the shop owners. When the shopkeeper stocked them, Forster employees would show up later to buy some.

5

Microwave

BORN IN 1894 AND ORPHANED BY THE AGE OF SEVEN, PERCY LEBARON SPENCER dropped out of his school in tiny Howland when he was twelve to help support his recently-widowed aunt, working in a spool mill from dawn to dark.

At sixteen, he learned a paper mill in town planned to introduce electricity, as yet barely known to rural areas. Spencer studied as much as he could about the concept, applied for work at the paper mill, and was one of three people assigned to install the electricity, despite a total lack of formal training.

When he was eighteen, Spencer joined the Navy, where he studied wireless and radio technology on his own while standing watch. He also taught himself trigonometry, calculus, chemistry, physics, and metallurgy.

Spencer went on to become one of the leading experts in the world on radar tube design and worked at Raytheon, where he helped the company win contracts to produce radar for the Massachusetts Institute of Technology. Employing magnetrons to generate the microwave radio signals for radar, Spencer figured out an efficient way to make magnetrons, increasing production greatly.

> One day Spencer was standing in front of an active radar set while he was building magnetrons, and he noticed that the candy bar in his pocket had melted. Apparently he was not the first to notice the phenomenon, but he was the first to pursue it. He began experimenting, using different foods, including popcorn and an egg. The popcorn popped, the egg exploded. .

Spencer created the first microwave oven by attaching a high density electromagnetic field to an enclosed metal box, which kept the microwaves from escaping.

On October 8, 1945, Spencer applied for a patent on his oven, which came to be called the Radarange. During his lifetime, this man with no formal education received 300 patents, earned the Distinguished Public Service Award from the U.S.

Navy for his magnetron work at Raytheon, had a building named after him at Raytheon Missile Defense Center in Woburn, Massachusetts, was awarded fellowship in the American Academy of Arts and Sciences, membership in the Institute of Radio Engineers, and an honorary Doctor of Science from the University of Massachusetts.

And for inventing the microwave oven while employed at Raytheon—Spencer received the usual $2 gratuity and no royalties. 🍁

The microwave oven did not become an overnight kitchen sensation since the first one measured about six feet tall, weighed 750 pounds, and cost upwards of $3,000. It was not until the late '60s that the size and price had shrunk to accommodate consumers' countertops and wallets.

Left: The Raytheon "Radar Range" aboard the NS *Savannah* nuclear-powered cargo ship, ca 1961.

24
Radar
Range

6

Doughnut Hole

CAPTAIN HANSON CROCKETT GREGORY WAS ONLY SIXTEEN, THE STORY GOES, when he invented the hole in the doughnut. Several variations of the story abound, and since it is nigh impossible to prove this long after the event on June 22, 1847, it will be up to you to decide.

Gregory, son of a comfortable shipping family from Rockport, claimed that at age sixteen, he cut the first hole in a doughnut before it was fried, thereby eliminating the center, which rarely cooked through and left a doughy mess inside. The hole allowed for the doughnut to cook evenly throughout.

In a more fanciful version of the tale, Gregory was enjoying a doughnut while at the helm of a sailing vessel. When a ferocious storm blew up he needed both hands to steer the boat. Gregory pushed his doughnut onto the spoke of the wheel, keeping the donut accessible, pushing out the doughy center, and creating the donut hole.

An even more fanciful version is that angels came to Gregory in a dream, suggesting the appropriate shape for a doughnut.

The most accepted version is that Gregory was at sea, but not yet a captain (that came later, when he was nineteen—Maine's youngest captain), when he was inspired to hollow out the doughnut's middle with a pepper box lid.

In an interview he gave the *Washington Post* in 1916, at age 85, he said he never liked the uncooked spots that occurred in *olykoeks*, the Dutch word for the precursor of the doughnut. These "dough knots" were diamond shaped twisted strips of dough (sort of pretzel shaped but without holes)—His mother, Elizabeth Gregory, was noted for making great olykoeks, flavoring them with nutmeg and other spices her son brought home from his voyages.

GREASY SINKERS

In yet another crazy tale, the heavy, doughy fried donuts were so dense and filling they slowed men at their work. After six men fell overboard and were so lethargic that they sank and drowned, Gregory began calling donuts, "greasy sinkers." Then he got the idea to cut out the centers to make them lighter and less filling.

In his own words, from the *Washington Post* story:

"Well, sir, they used to fry all right around the edges, but when you had the edges done the insides was all raw dough. And the twisters used to sop up all the grease just where they bent, and they were tough on the digestion.

"Well, I says to myself, 'Why wouldn't a space inside solve the difficulty?' I thought at first I'd take one of the strips and roll it around, then I got an inspiration, a great inspiration:

I took the cover off the ship's tin pepper box, and I cut into the middle of that doughnut the first hole ever seen by mortal eyes!"

[The next time he went home, he showed his mother this new method.]

"I says to her: 'Let me make some doughnuts for you.' She says, 'All right,' so I made her one or two and then showed her how.

"She then made several panfuls and sent them down to Rockland. Everybody was delighted and they never made doughnuts any other way except the way I showed my mother."

On the 100th anniversary of the doughnut hole, the town of Rockport honored its inventor with a plaque at the site of his birth. The house is gone, but the plaque can be seen on the south side of the Nativity Lutheran Church on Old County Road.

Seeds of Peace

IN 1993, AMERICAN JOURNALIST JOHN WALLACH HAD AN IDEA: WHAT IF CHILDREN from opposite sides of the Arab-Israeli conflict could become friends? Would the political situation in their region begin to change?

At a state dinner attended by Palestinian, Israeli, and Egyptian politicians, Wallach suggested they commit to sending fifteen teenagers from each nation to a summer camp he planned to open in Maine. They agreed.

That summer, 46 students ranging in age from 11 to 15, including three Americans, met in Otisfield, at Camp Powhatan. That fall, when the Oslo Accord was signed in Washington, D.C., the campers were invited to the White House and were in attendance as Israeli Prime Minister Yitzhak Rabin and Palestinian Liberation Organization Chairman Yasser Arafat signed the "Declaration of Principles on Interim Self-Government Arrangements."

"It was really difficult, especially to have people from the 'other side' next to me, sleeping with me. We are raised to hate them. So when you come here with that idea and hatred in your heart, and you come here and you find out they're actually people. They're nice."
—*Young Palestinian girl*

The roughly 300 campers who attend each year play games together, go swimming and canoeing, much like a regular summer camp. But then, are encouraged to express their feelings about the political conflicts they experience at home and learn from their counterparts on the other side. "Seeds" say it is not easy. They spend 110 minutes a day discussing the challenges of living in communities divided by conflict.

2009 Spring Seminar meeting between Palestinian, Israeli Arab and Jewish Israeli Seeds.

The objective is to provide students with the skills to become effective peacemakers back home, and to create a safe space while at camp for the young people to explore their feelings. There are daily news updates in the native languages of the students, so while they are attempting to break through to understanding each other, they are also working within the context of current events. Sometimes the teens find accord with their former enemies, but return home to be called traitors for fraternizing with them.

> "Teachers at my school asked us to say the first word that crosses our
> mind when we hear the word 'Palestinian'. Some said terrorists.
> Some said 'neighbors'. I said 'friends'."
>
> ——*Young Israeli girl*

Seeds of Peace offers leadership development programs for the Camp's alumni in their home countries. Though the camp is in Maine, Seeds of Peace administrative offices are headquartered in New York City. In 2000, the camp introduced a domestic session, initially for students from Maine, to help largely white communities adjust to an influx of immigrants, asylum seekers, and refugees from nations as diverse as Somalia and Cambodia. The program model in Maine was so successful that Seeds of Peace expanded it to include students from Syracuse, New York City, Los Angeles, and Chicago.

During the course of its existence, Seeds of Peace has expanded its sphere to include campers from other world conflict zones and has now graduated "Seeds" from Egypt, Palestine, Israel, Jordan, Morocco, Qatar, Tunisia, Afghanistan, Yemen, India, Pakistan, Cyprus, Turkey, Greece, Saudi Arabia, Iraq, Romania, Bulgaria, the United States, the United Kingdom and the Balkans (Albania, Croatia, Macedonia, Serbia, and Kosovo.)

The Earmuff

ON DECEMBER 4, 1858, CHESTER GREENWOOD WAS BORN INTO A POOR FAMILY OF SIX children in Farmington, Maine. He was well-known in town, even as a child, because he did whatever he could to help his family survive, including walking eight miles to sell eggs from the family hens.

When he was only fifteen years old, Greenwood decided he did not want his ears to freeze any more when he participated in his favorite pastime, ice skating. Apparently he was susceptible to frostbite on his ears and his ears itched too much when he wore the wool caps nearly everyone else wore. So he designed his own "ear warmer" and enlisted his grandmother to sew pads of beaver fur and flannel to a wire frame.

He was awarded patent #188,292 on March 13, 1877, and opened "The Shop," his factory in West Farmington soon after. By 1833, the factory was turning out 30,000 Greenwood Ear Protectors annually. The year before his death, in 1936, the business was still flourishing, turning out 400,000 earmuffs to be sold around the world. During World War I, his factory provided earmuffs for thousands of soldiers.

Greenwood held many patents—some say more than 100—and like many prolific inventors, didn't fit the mold of his times. He was an early devotee of healthy living. He ran a mile every morning and he and his wife exercised regularly. Sarah Isabel Greenwood was a supporter of women's suffrage. They were supporters of the Grange, proponents of public education, active in the Unitarian Church, and busy with

> Friends made fun of Chester and his ear warmers at first, but soon were asking him to make some for them. By age 19, he had patented the device and improved it, attaching the pads, now lined with velvet, to flat wire, and making them hinged for better fit and comfort.

The Chester Greenwood House in Farmington.

Every year, on the first Saturday of December, the town of Farmington celebrates Chester Greenwood Day. Besides a parade and other events, you can observe more varieties of earmuffs than can be imagined, perhaps even by Greenwood himself. Everyone, even spectators, is encouraged to sport earmuffs—the wilder the better.

other civic activities. He designed the home for their family of four children with many innovative architectural features. It still stands in Farmington.

Greenwood also ran a bicycle shop and a steam heating business, founded the first telephone company in Farmington (he even made all the receivers and transmitters himself). He partnered in a steamboat excursion business on Clearwater Lake. His machine shop was known for innovative solutions that included wheel grinders and self-priming spark plugs. He remained in Farmington until his death on July 5, 1937.

A mechanical genius, Greenwood's patents include a spring-tooth rake, a boring machine used in wood-turning, an advertising match box, a mechanical decoy mouse trap, a hook for pulling donuts out of the hot fat, a folding bed, bearings to keep wheels on axles, a "rubberless rubber band," a whistling tea kettle, and a fluid shock absorber. He is also credited with other inventions that he did not patent, such as a pipe vise, an umbrella holder, and a portable camp.

The Caterpillar Tread

AT THE END OF THE 19TH CENTURY MOST LOGS WERE HAULED AROUND THE WOODS in winter via sled pulled by oxen or horses and going downhill on snow or ice was a risky undertaking. Waterville blacksmith Alvin Orlando Lombard was invited by the president of a lumber company to solve the problem of getting logs out of the woods more easily and safely.

Already a mechanically-talented inventor with a few patents to his name, Lombard came up with a steam-driven tracked crawler in 1900 and applied for a patent after it was built for him by the Waterville Iron Works. He called it a "logging engine," and demonstrated it on Thanksgiving Day in 1900.

As with many inventions of the time, Lombard was not the first to envision a machine with treads to haul heavy loads in difficult terrain. Warren P. Miller of Marysville, California, received a patent for a tracked vehicle to run on dirt in 1859, but he never manufactured it. That patent had expired by the time Lombard built his machine, and it's unlikely Lombard even knew about it.

The steam-driven continuous track quickly revolutionized the logging industry. Almost overnight the crawlers became popular throughout the Maine and New Hampshire woods and into Canada. In 1909, Lombard built a gasoline-powered version, which replaced the steam vehicles by 1917, even though they had less power. He tried a diesel-powered log hauler in 1917, but by then, trucks could run on woods roads cleared by bulldozers and the single-purpose log hauler became obsolete.

Most of the 83 Lombard steam machines known to have been constructed were used in Maine and New Hampshire, although a few were purchased for use in Michigan,

> The Lombard Steam Log Hauling Company was the first manufacturer of a successful "tractor crawler" using what is now known as a "tank tread" or "caterpillar track," defined as a system of propulsion using a continuous band of treads or track plates, driven by two or more wheels.

Lombard Log Hauler #38, built ca. 1910, restored in 2014 by the University of Maine Mechanical Engineering Technology class of 2014 and the Maine Forest and Logging Museum.

A restored Lombard steam log hauler at Clark's Trading Post in Lincoln, New Hampshire.

Wisconsin, and Russia. Some of the steam-driven haulers were reportedly still in use until 1929. The Maine State Museum displays a gasoline-powered Lombard and several others are displayed intact in various logging museums and other places in Maine and a few other states.

The track system became the basis for the success of tanks in World War I and all future wars. In Antarctica, the highest peak in the mountain mass near Cape Sobral is named Mount Lombard, and in 1982, a Lombard Steam Log Hauler was designated a National Historic Mechanical Engineering Landmark.

THE NAME IN EARTH MOVING

California tractor manufacturer Benjamin Holt, bought another tractor company, renamed the new company Caterpillar Traction Company and moved it to Peoria, Illinois. There the company began manufacturing tractors that utilized the track covered by the Lombard patent.

Lombard traveled to California in 1910 and requested payment for the use of his patent. Holt agreed and asked Lombard to send a contract, but Holt never signed it and never paid any royalty. Holt's company, now known simply as Caterpillar, Inc., has become a world leader in the manufacture of earth-moving equipment.

In many resources, Holt is identified as the inventor of the track, primarily because the name Caterpillar came to represent the track after Holt copyrighted it. Holt received a patent in 1912, but it was for a different suspension method, not for the underlying principle.

The Holt 75 model gasoline-powered Caterpillar tractor used early in World War I as an artillery tractor. Later models were produced without the front "tiller wheel."

Photographic Dry Plate

THE STANLEY BROTHERS, IDENTICAL TWINS FRANCIS EDGAR AND FREELAN OSCAR, were born June 1, 1849 in Kingfield, on the shores of the wild Carrabasset River. Frank and Freel, or F.E. and F.O., as the brothers were variously called, showed their genius at an early age. Despite their precocity, no one could have predicted they would become prolific inventors and financially successful businessmen.

By age seven they were whittling small animal figures. At age ten, F.O. carved a child-size violin and taught himself to play. By their mid-teens, both boys were carving and playing violins. One of their several successful businesses as adults was the manufacture of violins that were highly praised by musicians, including a Boston Symphony Orchestra violinist who prized his Stanley violin as highly as his Stradivarius.

Neither ever drank alcohol or caffeine. They grew to be six feet tall, looked exactly alike, and reveled in playing tricks on the local constabulary and others.

F.O. left school when he experienced his first bout with tuberculosis. The twins later married and went their separate ways, living in different towns for a few years. F.E. ended up in Auburn, where, in addition to teaching school, he began drawing portraits for people. He realized it would be easier if he could use photographs and work on the portraits at home.

Photography was in its infancy, and the glass plates used in the large-format cameras had to be used wet, with the chemicals applied in the field at the time of the shoot. These plates often failed, or burned up, and although many people had experimented with using dry plates, none had yet been successful.

In a move typical of the Stanleys, who rarely settled for an inferior
product if they thought they could improve it, F.E. decided to
create a reliable dry plate— and so he did.

F. O. & F. E. STANLEY.

MACHINE FOR MANUFACTURING PHOTOGRAPHIC DRY PLATES.

No. 345,331. Patented July 13, 1886.

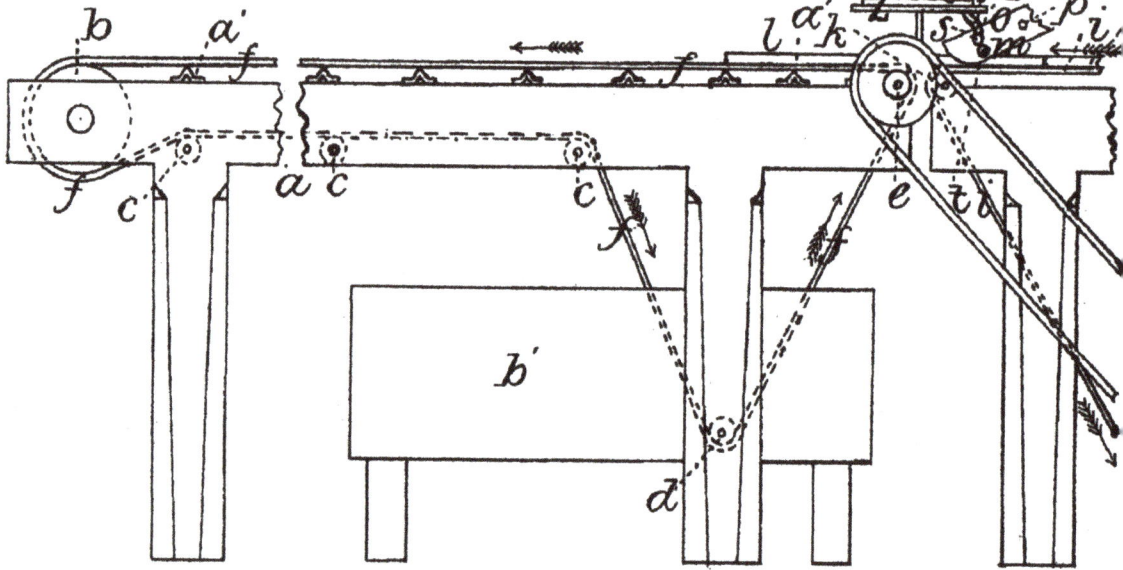

FIG.1.

Patent diagram of the Stanleys' machine for manufacturing their dry photographic plates.

Calling on F.O. to join him in his Auburn business in 1884, the twins reunited, and made plates by hand in their new Stanley Dry Plate Company. In 1886, F.O. designed a machine to help the brothers mass-produce the plates. The patent for this device is the only one of hundreds of patents they held together in which F.O.'s name appears first.

The business was quickly and wildly successful, prompting them to move closer to Boston. They settled in Newton and established their company there in 1890. Their fame spread to the Eastman-Kodak Company in Rochester, New York, where George

Eastman had been trying for years to develop a workable dry plate. The superior Stanley plate was outselling Eastman's by far.

Eastman tried everything to acquire the Stanleys' plate formula, starting with offering to buy their company. The twins absolutely refused to sell. Rumor has it that Eastman even tried to steal the formula, unsuccessfully.

Meanwhile, the brothers, also amateur architects, were making so much money they could spend more time designing houses and raising race horses. They designed their own homes in Newton, and homes and a school in their native Kingfield.

The company's motto was: "On! Stanley, On!" and eventually, after becoming so busy with their newer venture, the Stanley Steamer automobile, the brothers decided to move on and sell the company to Eastman.

> "Maybe we ought to sell the dry plate company to Eastman. I think he's earned it," said F.E. to F.O. one day. "He'll know he earned it when he hears the asking price," responded F.O.

The price was never revealed but it was rumored to be an astronomical figure for the era—around $600,000. Eastman snapped it up, and it's a major reason the most famous name in American photographic film is Eastman Kodak, and not Stanley. The successful dry plate revolutionized the photo industry worldwide.

The frugal Yankee brothers rarely made financial mistakes, but they admitted to one: Part of the sale price was stock in Eastman Kodak, which the brothers sold back to Eastman within a year. A few years later that stock was worth millions.

F.E. and F.O.'s sister, Chansonetta Stanley Emmons, was a photographer in her own right whose work depicts scenes of everyday life and the rural landscape of New England. In the 1970s, the director of the Farnsworth Museum in Rockland found a cache of Chansonetta's dry plates in the museum basement. He had them printed and produced a book of her life and photographs in 1977—*Chansonetta: The Life and Photographs of Chansonetta Stanley Emmons, 1858-1937*—finally giving her the recognition critics believe she deserved.

In 1951, the Freeport store, then the only Bean retail store, began staying open 24 hours a day so hunters and fishermen traveling from around the country could stop in anytime to get their equipment en route to their Maine destination. It has only closed a few times—two Sundays in 1962 during a state "Blue Laws" change, for the death of President John F. Kennedy in 1963, and for the death of L.L. Bean himself in 1967.

The giant replica Bean boot outside the L.L. Bean flagship store in Freeport is the equivalent to a shoe size 410.

The Bean Boot

LEON LEONWOOD (L.L.) BEAN WAS AN AVID HUNTER, FISHERMAN, AND GENERAL OUT-doorsman in a state with a lot of outdoors to explore, including thousands of freshwater bodies of water and more than 12 million acres of woods.

Bean had a problem, however. He often returned from a hunting trip with cold, wet feet. In 1911, he decided to do something about it. Bean asked a cobbler to stitch leather boot tops onto workmen's rubber boots to make a boot that could keep his feet warm and dry during his slogs through the Maine woods.

It worked, and Bean figured other outdoorsmen might like to have dry feet as well. So in 1912, he acquired a list of out-of-state hunting license holders and sent them all a flyer advertising his Maine Hunting Shoe and guaranteeing "perfect satisfaction in every way." His appeal was convincing and Bean immediately received 100 orders. Unfortunately, in 90 of the first 100 pairs, the uppers separated from the bottoms and they were returned. His fledgling business nearly ended there, but true to his word, he sent a refund to every dissatisfied purchaser.

Working out of the basement of his brother's clothing store in Freeport, he borrowed more money, started over, and fixed the problem.

> Bean learned that he should test his products personally and
> that customer satisfaction was paramount to success.

By 1951, the store was stocking specialized outdoor wear for hunting and fishing, fishing rods and flies, snowshoes, rifles, and all manner of other equipment vital to the outdoor adventurer. In the '70s, backpackers and campers joined the ranks of avid Bean customers. The flagship store still stands in the same downtown Freeport location as the tiny store Bean opened in 1917, but it has grown many times. Now 200,000 square feet, the store includes an indoor trout pond and a 3,500-gallon aquarium. The seven-acre campus also includes three other specialized Bean stores and lots of parking.

While there is a difference now between the original Maine Hunting Shoe and another Bean Boot actually called by that name, the names are interchangeable to most folks and there are dozens of heights and materials from which to choose. However, they are all identifiable as a Bean boot since the styles are so similar save for color and height. While the company's products are sourced from all over the world, the Bean boot is still manufactured in Freeport, as are the signature canvas tote bags.

Three things have not changed besides the look of the Bean boot: 1) Employees still field-test products to insure their quality, 2) The customer service for which L.L. Bean is known throughout the retail industry and the country, and 3) Bean's original guarantee of customer satisfaction is still intact since he launched the policy in 1912.

As testament to the success of the boot that launched a retail empire, at the entrance to the flagship store in Freeport stands a giant replica of a Bean boot. Bean officials say it would be a size 410. There is also a small fleet of "bootmobiles"—cars in the shape of a Bean boot—that are used to promote the brand.

Granite

FROM ITALY, FINLAND, SCOTLAND, SWEDEN, AND OTHER PARTS OF EUROPE THEY came in the early 1800s, experienced stonecutters to extract Maine's abundant supply of granite, mostly from quarries along the coast and on some islands.

The stone, which came in many hues depending on the region, was used to construct important buildings from New York City to San Francisco and New Orleans. Many Maine residents who worked in or even lived near a quarry could recognize the stone from their local enterprise when they spotted a granite building while traveling.

Granite is an igneous rock that gains its different colors by the mixture of quartz and feldspar contained in it. Feldspar comes in many colors, such as pink, white, or tan, while quartz crystals can be clear or hazy, and like the mica also found in granite, ranges from white to black. If granite is black, that means it contains

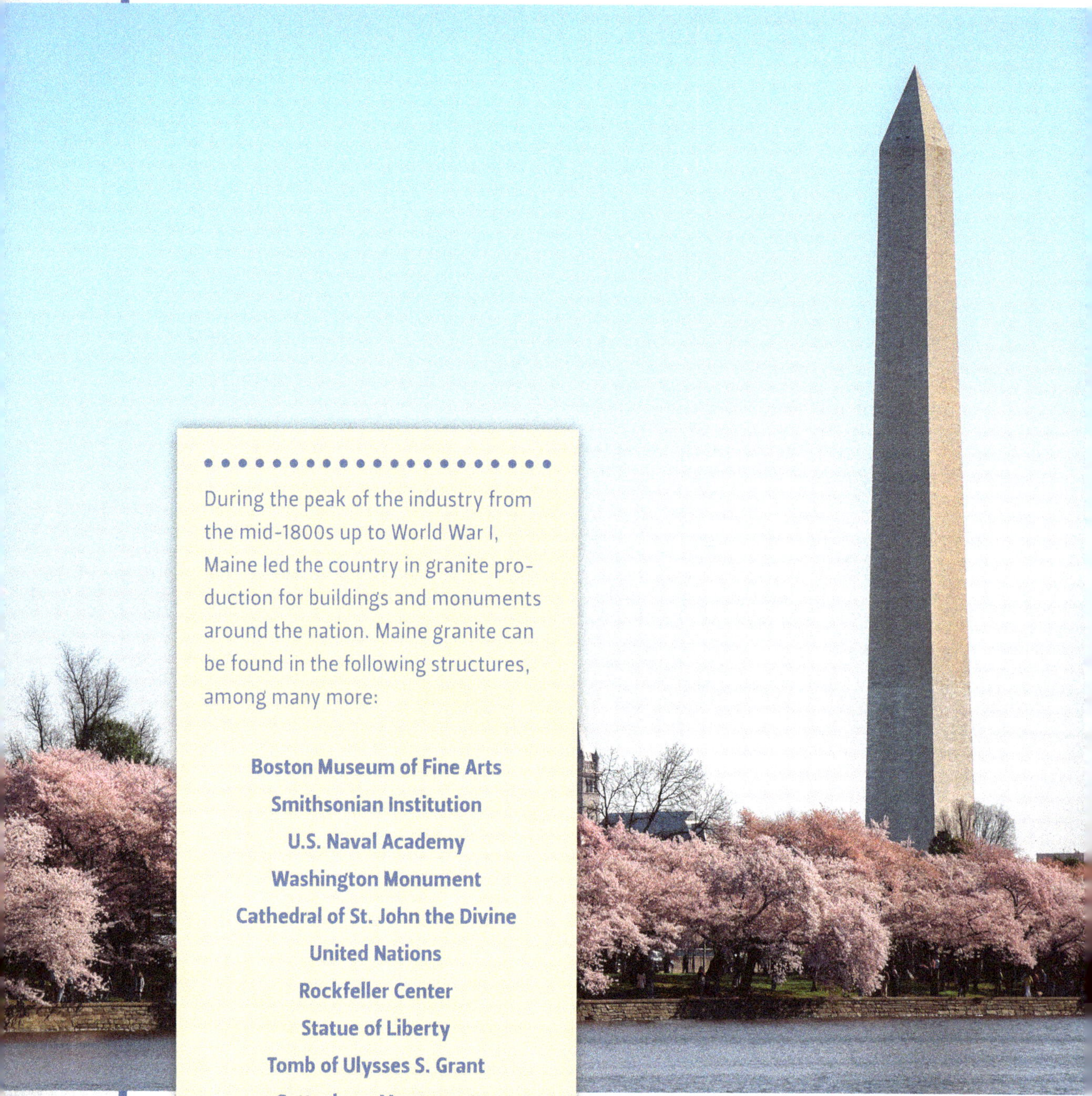

During the peak of the industry from the mid-1800s up to World War I, Maine led the country in granite production for buildings and monuments around the nation. Maine granite can be found in the following structures, among many more:

Boston Museum of Fine Arts

Smithsonian Institution

U.S. Naval Academy

Washington Monument

Cathedral of St. John the Divine

United Nations

Rockfeller Center

Statue of Liberty

Tomb of Ulysses S. Grant

Gettysburg Monument

The Washington Monument in Washington, D.C. contains significant amounts of Maine granite.

a high amount of hornblende. At some Maine quarry sites, the granite runs five miles deep. Granite was quarried by workers who drilled holes perpendicular to the stone's grain and used dynamite, steam drills, splitting wedges, and hammers to break off slabs or blocks.

> One square inch of the strongest granite can endure 32,635 pounds without breaking, while the "crushing strength" of iron is a mere 3,000 pounds per square inch.

In the early days, granite was usually quarried to create sturdy underpinnings for bridges, breakwaters, and buildings, but as the 19th century rush to create memorable, permanent buildings increased, granite, with hues ranging from pink and lavender to beige and black, moved above ground for beautiful facades, columns, steps, and other structural pieces.

Maine's granite industry peaked at around 170 quarries, with 153 active in 1895 alone. Most were located along the coast from St. George to Deer Isle. Construction with granite was gradually eliminated when lower-cost concrete was introduced in the early 1900s. Some of the quarries shut down virtually overnight, leaving abandoned communities and piles of granite by the shore. One such huge pile is clearly visible in St. George.

If the quarries are gone, their products live on all over the country as monuments to the industry, and in the last names and customs of Maine families who can trace their origins to the stonecutters of old.

A quarry on Crotch Island, near Deer Isle, supplied the stone for President Kennedy's memorial in Arlington National Cemetery. Jacqueline Kennedy traveled to the island to select the stone personally. This is the only quarry in Maine still working, supplying mostly decorative items such as markers or countertops from granite often described as lavender-hued.

The useful beauty of the single-masted design of the Friendship sloop enabled a solo lobster-
man to sail the boat and haul traps without help; although the vessels were used for all kinds of
fishing, such as herring seining, hand-lining for cod, and mackerel and swordfishing.

Years ago, an old fisherman recalled how to handle the Friendship sloop when sailing alone:
"Lead out the sheet of the mains'l quite a way, and trim the jib tight while you're hauling. The
sloop will lay good then."

Friendship Sloop

DESIGNED SO MAINE'S LOBSTER HARVESTERS COULD SAIL THEIR VESSEL SINGLE- handedly, the gracious Friendship sloop has earned a permanent place among beautiful boats. Also known as the Muscongus Bay sloop, or just the lobster sloop, the design emerged around 1880 in mid-coast Maine. Influenced by the fishing schooners of Gloucester, Massachusetts, it soon became the vessel of choice for most lobstermen.

This gaff-rigged sloop started out between 16 and 20 feet long, allowing for large loads yet providing comfort in a small forward cabin with bunks and a stove. Later, the boats became larger, averaging 30 to 40 feet in their heyday.

Friendship, Maine, boatbuilder Wilbur A. Morse built many of the vessels through 1910 and a lot of his boats are still afloat, lovingly restored. Although many other builders produced the craft along the Maine coast, Morse's name stands out because of the high numbers he produced. The boat's name eventually evolved from the town where his shop was located.

The usual building method involved men cutting their own wood and hauling it to the sawmill with horses. A fisherman might build his own boat over the winter, fish with it all summer, sell it in the fall, then build another. People continue to have Friendship sloops built as pleasure craft, often of fiberglass now, although some are still made of wood.

A lesser vessel might have disappeared with the advent of gasoline-powered motors, but the craft's beauty attracted yachtsmen and pleasure boaters. In 1961, a Massachusetts sailor launched a homecoming race in the town of Friendship, from which the Friendship Sloop Society formed. Friendship is a small town, so by the 1980s, the celebration had overwhelmed it. Now the event is held in nearby Rockland. Every summer, the society holds regattas in Maine, Connecticut, and Massachusetts.

> While Friendship sloops are not exactly the same in all respects, they do look alike and share some design features in common: They are single-masted, gaff-rigged, with a mainsail and staysail, and usually a jib. They have a full keel, an elliptical stern, and a bowsprit. Another common feature: The first view of an elegant, graceful Friendship sloop is arresting, often breathtaking.

Sealed Dive Suit

LEONARD NORCROSS IS ONE OF THOSE MOSTLY SELF-TAUGHT INVENTORS WHO overcame early personal adversity to acquire several patents for mechanical devices and to achieve stature as a lecturer.

Norcross was born in 1798 in Readfield. His father died when he was three and, although he lived with his mother, she eventually apprenticed him to a rather mean farmer. Norcross left the farmer after three years to live with his aunt in Greene, where he was able to attend school and learned to be a millwright. He taught for a few years, then went to work in a saw mill.

Early on, he displayed an aptitude for mechanical things. After the saw mill, he moved to Dixfield, where he began inventing various machines and received several patents.

His most lasting invention was the first successful airtight, underwater diving suit—the first with a closed helmet connected via a rubber hose to an air pump on a boat above the diver. He called his suit "diving armor," and it was made of leather, with lead-weighted feet, and a brass helmet with a pressure valve. When the watertight joint that connected the hose with the helmet was closed, the suit filled with air. Exhaust air exited out the top of the helmet.

Other patents attributed to Norcross included a threshing and separating machine, a nail-making machine, an accelerated spinner for wool, and a stump lifter. A biographer claims one Norcross invention was mistakenly filed under someone else's name and that Norcross was defrauded of his rights in that instance.

A well-rounded man, in addition to his inventions, Norcross also preached the gospel and lectured on astronomy and temperance. He died in Dixfield on March 10, 1865.

Patent # 8255 was issued to Norcross on June 14, 1834. Though an Englishman had previously invented a dive suit, it had greatly restricted the diver's movements. Norcross's invention enabled divers to move freely for the first time, to bend over, or even to lie down underwater. In honor of his achievement, Norcross named his son Submarinus.

U.S. NAVY STANDARD
DIVING APPARATUS

15

Airbrush

THE TWIN STANLEY BROTHERS WERE PROLIFIC INVENTORS BEST KNOWN FOR the Stanley Steamer and the dry plate photographic process. This precocious pair invented many things, often to enhance or make something they were doing more efficient. Usually their patents bore both names; and Francis Edgar's name was usually listed first because they were primarily his idea.

The airbrush, however, was exclusively F.E.'s invention. After they finished school and each married, the brothers briefly went their separate ways. While teaching school in Strong, Francis began to paint a few portraits for fun. He entered and won a state-wide crayon portrait contest and decided to launch a professional career.

**The airbrush changed the arts in 1876,
and it's still in use . . .**

One reason F.E. Stanley's invention of the airbrush may often be overlooked is that he never produced the device for sale—he merely wanted it for his own use. He also may not have gotten around to selling it because the portrait-painting business led quickly to the photography business, which entailed producing a better photographic plate and another patent for the brothers.

He and his wife moved to Auburn, where F.E. went door-to-door, asking people if they wanted their portraits drawn. One of the doors he knocked on belonged to the publisher of the local daily newspaper, the *Lewiston Sun*, who suggested that F.E. place some portraits in the windows of the local art store to attract business. So he did.

Soon he had all the drawing work he could handle. True to form, he wasn't satisfied, and in 1876, at age 27, F.E. received Patent Number 182,389. It wasn't called the airbrush at the time, but a "paint distributor" or "atomizer." However, it was a device that used compressed air to apply liquid color smoothly to flat surfaces. In many

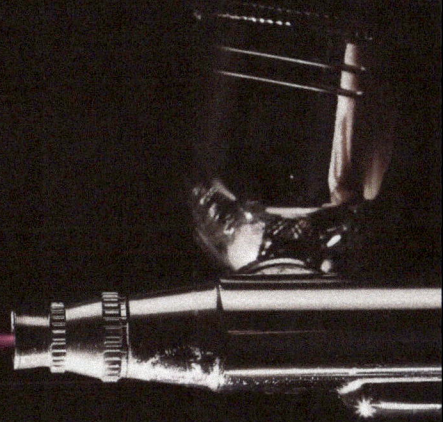

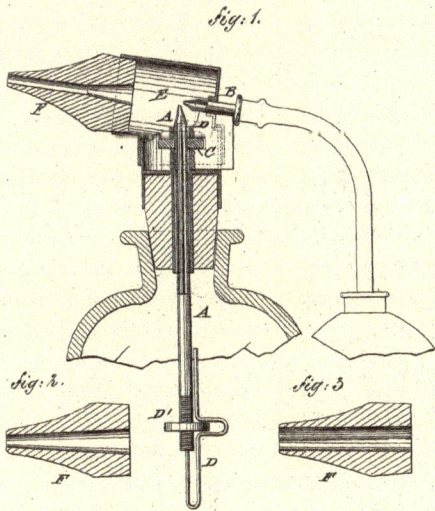

F. E. STANLEY.
ATOMIZERS.

No. 182,389.

Patented Sept. 19, 1876.

fig. 1.

fig. 2.

fig. 3.

WITNESSES:
Chas. Nate
John Goddale

INVENTOR:
F. E. Stanley
BY
ATTORNEYS.

accounts of the invention of the airbrush, F.E.'s patent is overlooked and Abner Peeler is credited with making the first device, but Peeler really only made changes to the invention for his 1879 patent.

In some of the accounts where Stanley is rightly credited with the first invention, readers are informed that no existing pictures exist where the Stanley device was used. Wrong again. Originals of F.E. Stanley's airbrushed portraits are on display at the Stanley Museum in Kingfield. The building was designed, built, and donated by the Stanley brothers (who also happened to be architects in their spare time) to be used as a school in their home town. On display in the museum are Stanley Steamers and many artifacts, pictures, and documents that record their illustrious careers.

Prohibition

AMERICA'S FIRST TEMPERANCE SOCIETY WAS FOUNDED IN PORTLAND IN 1815. By 1834, temperance societies from around the state had banded together, gaining political clout. Neal S. Dow, a Portland native from a Quaker family, was a zealous reformer and stood staunchly against "demon rum."

Dow was active in the cause that blamed alcohol for many of society's ills. He was elected president of the Maine Temperance Union in 1850, and then elected Mayor of Portland the next year. By 1851, he had gained enough influence to persuade Governor John Hubbard to sign a law totally banning the sale or manufacture of liquor in the state. The "Maine Law" quickly became famous across the country and several other states passed similar laws.

Had it not been for the start of the Civil War, a national ban on alcoholic beverages might have happened sooner. However, by 1919, the Eighteenth Amendment to the U.S. Constitution mandated a nationwide prohibition on alcohol.

Dow enforced the Maine Law with vigor, exacting harsh penalties for violations, which made him extremely unpopular, especially with poor folks and immigrants. In 1855, his opponents stormed Portland City Hall because they'd heard Dow was keeping liquor in the basement of a public building—Dow did indeed have a stash of alcohol, but it was legal and intended for doctors and pharmacists.

Dow ordered the state militia to fire on the crowd. One man was killed and seven injured in what came to be known as the Portland Rum Riot. The riot helped repeal the law in 1856, but it kept getting re-enacted and was eventually written into the state constitution in 1885. Dow's mayoral career ended as a result of the riot when he chose not to run again. He was elected to the legislature for two terms, but an unconnected financial scandal ended his political career.

Dow emerged from the Civil War a brigadier general, and spent his time through the 1860s and 1870s giving speeches promoting temperance across the U.S., Canada, and Great Britain. He quit the Republican party to join the new Prohibitionist party, whose votes in New York played spoiler, costing Maine Republican James G. Blaine the presidency in 1884. That same year, Dow ran in the Portland mayoral election on the Prohibition ticket and lost.

A year later, he gave his last speech, criticizing Portland for failing to adequately enforce the prohibition laws. He began writing, but never finished a memoir entitled *The Reminiscences of Neal Dow: Recollections of Eighty Years*. Guess all that temperance paid off for Dow. On his death in 1897, he was 93 years old.

The Maine Law was heralded internationally and inspired the United Kingdom Alliance in Manchester, England, where a street called "Dog Kennel Lane" was renamed "Maine Road" in honor of the temperance movement.

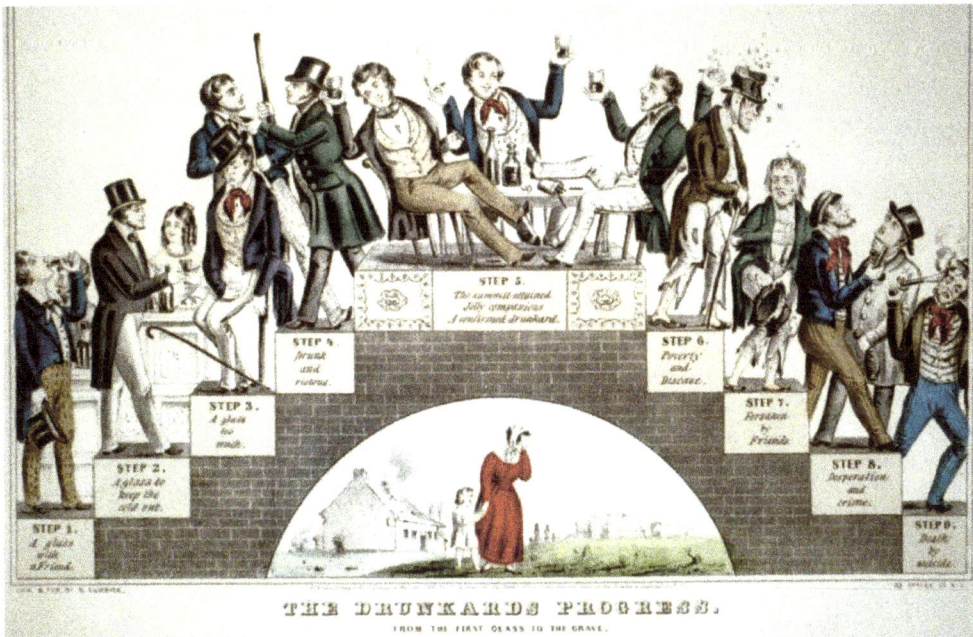

THE DRUNKARDS PROGRESS.
FROM THE FIRST GLASS TO THE GRAVE.

Mitchell said that he acquired an extra measure of an already plentiful supply of patience while serving as Senate president for six years, which he described as "the toughest job in the western world," because "a lot of what happens in the Senate is delay for the sake of delay, obstruction for the sake of obstruction."

George Mitchell

GEORGE JOHN MITCHELL, JR., WAS BORN IN WATERVILLE ON AUGUST 20, 1933. HIS father, who worked as a janitor at Colby College, was an orphan of Irish descent adopted and raised by a Lebanese family. His mother Mary emigrated from Bkassine, Lebanon, in 1920 and worked in a Waterville textile mill. They had five children, four boys and a girl. Raised as a Maronite Catholic, Mitchell is recognized as a prominent Arab-American. He graduated high school at age 16, attended Bowdoin College, then served in the U.S. Army as an intelligence officer for two years.

Mitchell then attended Georgetown University Law Center's part-time night program to earn his law degree. After a stint at the Department of Justice, he served as an executive assistant to Senator Edmund S. Muskie, a prominent Maine Democrat. This experience launched Mitchell's interest in politics.

> In the 1988 Senate race, George Mitchell was re-elected with 81 percent of the vote, a record margin for a Maine senator that still stands.

While practicing law in Portland, Mitchell decided to run for governor of Maine, winning the Democratic nomination but losing the election to Maine's first independent governor, James Longley, in a three-way race. In 1977 he was appointed as a federal judge to the U.S. District Court in Maine. Then in 1980, Governor Joseph Brennan appointed him to fill Muskie's Senate seat when Muskie was chosen as President Jimmy Carter's Secretary of State.

When that term expired, Mitchell was elected to the Senate seat in 1982, then re-elected, and re-elected again until 1994, when he decided not to run again. During his Senate tenure, including serving as majority leader, he was credited with leading the movement to reauthorize the Clean Air Act and pass the Americans with Disabilities Act. For six consecutive years he was voted by his fellow senators as their most respected member.

To continue his efforts to pass meaningful health care legislation, Mitchell turned down President Bill Clinton's offer of an appointment to the Supreme Court in 1994.

Mitchell was also known for working closely with Maine's Republican Senator, Bill Cohen. Their Senate era marked the end of any significant congressional bipartisanship.

After he left the Senate, Mitchell was tapped in 1995 by President Clinton to serve as U.S. Special Envoy for Northern Ireland. He had never been to Northern Ireland before he began his work as peace broker and famously said that for the first six months, he couldn't understand a word anyone said. Although "The Troubles" had been a guerrilla civil war for

Mitchell, together with Benjamin Netanyahu, Mahmoud Abbas, and Hillary Clinton at the start of Middle East talks on September 2, 2010.

thirty years, the political animosity, religious divisiveness, and resentment had been simmering for much longer, and was exacerbated when the south achieved independence and created the Irish Republic in 1922.

Despite a near-collapse of talks after two years of negotiation, Mitchell persevered, finally getting all sides to agree to a two-week timetable with small daily goals. Finally, in 1998 the momentous Belfast Peace Agreement, also known as the Good Friday Agreement, was reached, a testimony to Mitchell's patience and negotiating abilities. For his success, he was awarded the Presidential Medal of Freedom and the Liberty Medal.

"I had no power. All I had was the power of persuasion."
—*George Mitchell writing about his experience with Belfast Peace Agreement in his book,* The Negotiator

After Ireland, Mitchell served as a special envoy to the Middle East, a partner in a prestigious D.C. law firm, chairman of the board of directors at Disney, and an investigator into steroid use in baseball.

Margaret Chase Smith

AT FIRST GLANCE, MARGARET CHASE SMITH SEEMS AN UNLIKELY WARRIOR. SHE WAS the only woman in the U.S. Senate when Joe McCarthy was conducting his infamous House Un-American Activities Committee hearings, finding Communists under every rock and destroying the careers of innocent Americans. And she was the first senator to openly oppose McCarthy on the Senate floor.

Margaret Chase was born December 14, 1897, in Skowhegan, in rural central Maine. After graduating from high school, she taught briefly at a one-room school, coached girls' high school basketball, worked at the telephone company, and finally became circulation manager at the town's newspaper.

That job changed her life—she married the paper's owner, Clyde Smith, 21 years her senior, in 1930. She began a busy life of community activity and political involvement, co-founding the Skowhegan chapter of the Business and Professional Women's Club and being elected to the Maine Republican State Committee.

In 1936, Clyde Smith was elected to the U.S. House of Representatives. Margaret moved with him to Washington, D.C. to serve as his secretary—a job that included research, speech-writing, and correspondence.

Clyde suffered a heart attack in 1940 and remained seriously ill afterward. He urged Margaret to run for his seat and issued a press release praising her experience and knowledge. When he died that spring, a special election was held for the remainder of his term. With no challenger, she won easily and became the first woman elected to Congress from Maine.

> Smith was a staunch supporter of the U.S. military. Her 1961 strong opposition to proposed reductions in defense and support for using nuclear weapons against the Soviets had the Kremlin calling her "an Amazon warmonger hiding behind a rose." Her response was, "Some Amazon. I'm five foot three."

This was the first of her many firsts. When the term ended, she defeated a Democratic challenger for the next two-year term, and was re-elected with at least 60 percent of the vote three more times.

Her interest in military issues brought her to the House Naval Affairs Committee, where she became the first civilian woman to travel on a U.S. Navy ship during World War II, taking a 25,000-mile tour of South Pacific bases. A strong supporter of women in the armed services, she introduced legislation that earned her the nickname "Mother of the WAVES."

Always a moderate and true to her Maine independent streak, she often voted against her party. She supported much of President Roosevelt's New Deal and was a strong supporter of Harry Truman's foreign policy. In the Senate she voted against two of President Eisenhower's Supreme Court picks.

When a longtime Maine senator retired in 1948, Smith ran for his seat, facing incumbent Governor Horace A. Hildreth, former Governor Sumner Sewall, and a minister in the primary. She won the primary, garnering more votes than the other three combined, and went on to defeat her Democratic rival with 71 percent of the vote. She was the first woman elected to the Senate from Maine and the first woman to serve in both houses of Congress.

> "Don't change a record for a promise."
> — *Margaret Chase Smith's campaign slogan*

Margaret Chase Smith had served in the Senate only one year, when, despite her early support for him, and her own anti-Communist views, she became disillusioned with Senator Joseph McCarthy's thin evidence for his accusations that many Communists worked in the State Department. In 1950, she addressed the Senate and became the first senator to denounce McCarthy's actions without naming him, saying the

Senate was "debased" by character assassination. Her bravery in defending what she called "some of the basic principles of Americanism: The right to criticize; The right to hold unpopular beliefs; The right to protest; The right of independent thought." attracted six other moderate senators to sign onto her declaration.

> **"I don't want to see the Republican Party ride to political victory on the four horsemen of calumny—fear, ignorance, bigotry and smear."**
> —*Margaret Chase Smith, from her "Declaration of Conscience."*

In retaliation, McCarthy removed her from the Permanent Subcommittee on Investigations, replacing her with Senator Richard Nixon. McCarthy also referred to her and the other signers of her Declaration as "Snow White and the Six Dwarves." Smith never flinched and her courage paid off. Although McCarthy continued his retaliation, supporting a rival candidate when she ran for re-election in 1954, he failed to unseat her, showing that he had been weakened politically. In 1954, the Senate censured McCarthy.

Her opposition to McCarthy, however, may have cost her the chance to be Dwight Eisenhower's running mate. Instead, he chose Nixon. In 1960, she defeated a strong Democratic Maine woman to retain her Senate seat. This was another first—the first time two women competed for the Senate.

In 1964, she decided to run for president—the first woman from a major party to launch a presidential campaign, and the first woman to have her name placed in nomination at a national convention—but she failed to win the nomination.

From her early days in the House, Smith began to wear a single red rose every day and started a long campaign to recognize the rose as the country's official flower. The rose was adopted, but not until 1987. The morning after President John F. Kennedy was assassinated, Smith showed up before all the other senators and laid a single red rose on his former Senate desk.

Long wildly popular in Maine, she lost her Senate seat to Democrat William Hathaway in 1972, perhaps due to rumors of ill health and criticism that she had lost touch with Maine since she had no field office there. It was the only election she ever lost. Until 1981, she held the Senate record for consecutive roll-call votes with 2,941. She was also the first and so far, only, woman to serve as chair of the Senate Republican Conference. Margaret Chase Smith died in Skowhegan in 1995 at age 97.

19

Stephen King

STEPHEN KING IS INTERNATIONALLY KNOWN AS "THE KING OF HORROR," AND IS one of the world's all-time best-selling novelists, with sales exceeding 350 million. Many of his books have been made into feature films or mini-series. Seven of his 54 works of fiction were written under the nom de plume Richard Bachman, starting in 1977, because publishers believed the public would not accept more than one book a year from the same author. His fiction is not limited to horror, but also includes fantasy, science fiction, and western genres. The prolific King has also written some 200 short stories, screenplays, novellas, essays, columns, at least one musical play in collaboration with musician John Mellancamp, and a collaborative comic book series.

Many of King's books are set in his home state and several fictional towns have become famous as a result, such as Chamberlain, Derry, Chester's Mills, Haven, and Ludlow. But King was born in the very real city of Portland in 1947. Deserted by his father at age two, his mother moved King and his older brother to three states before returning to settle in Durham, Maine, when he was 11. He has lived in Maine ever since, except for one year when he moved his wife and children to Colorado.

Writing is King's primary vocation, but he loves music and has an intermittent rock band, the Rock Bottom Remainders. The band, whose name

King's home near downtown Bangor is a popular tourist attraction for people from around the globe. On nearly any day, people may be seen having their photo taken in front of his large red Victorian home with the custom-made 270-foot wrought iron fence, embellished appropriately with bats, gargoyles and a large spider web motif. Besides Bangor, he and his wife, Tabitha, maintain a home in Lovell, Maine, and winter in Sarasota, Florida.

is based on the term used for books sold at reduced prices, consists of amateur musicians who are published writers and their performances raise money for charity.

Political activism is another of King's avocations. He is passionately outspoken on behalf of liberal causes and candidates. He has often said rich Americans like himself should pay a higher tax rate, and he has called for increased gun control.

The Stephen and Tabitha King Foundation and their Barking Foundation distribute around $4 million a year to libraries, fire departments, schools, and assorted arts organizations. They have donated matching funds through their radio station, WKIT-FM, owned by their Zone Corporation, to help with heating bills of needy Bangor residents.

King was struck by a van while walking along a rural road in Lovell in 1999, causing him to suffer a collapsed lung, a broken hip, multiple fractures and lacerations, requiring multiple operations. His recuperation was long, slow, and painful. Although he had resumed writing, in 2002 he announced he would stop. Since that announcement, however, he has written several novels, a short story collection, and does not appear to be slowing down.

20

Ed Muskie

EDMUND MUSKIE, WAS AND DID MANY THINGS, BUT ONE OF THE MOST IMPORTANT things he did was display a talent for quiet leadership. Throughout his career, he was a true statesman who might have been the poster child for the concept of leading from behind.

Muskie was a Democrat in a hugely Republican state and he is credited with bringing the Democratic Party to the forefront in Maine. After serving in the Maine legislature, he ran for governor in 1955 and served two terms—he was Maine's first Catholic governor. During one term, the state legislature had a 4-1 ratio of Republicans to Democrats, but Muskie managed to pass the majority of his platform due to his ability to listen, reason, and persuade. After this, he was elected to the U.S. Senate and served from 1959 to 1980. In each of his three elections to the Senate, he won with more than 60 percent of the vote..

Muskie's father moved to the U.S. from Poland in 1903, changed his family name from Marciszewski to Muskie, and opened a tailor shop in Rumford. Ed was born on March 28, 1914. He was a shy child, but scholarly. Valedictorian of his high school class, he went on to study at Bates College on scholarship, where he was an athlete, a member of the debate team, and a member of student government, while also working several jobs. He graduated Phi Beta Kappa at the head of his class.

After college, he attended law school at Cornell, passed the Maine bar, and took over a small law practice in Waterville before serving in the Navy during World War II. When he returned from the war, he won a seat in the Maine House of Representatives.

Muskie was tall, rangy, direct, and well-known for his candor and integrity. In the tumultuous political year of 1968, Muskie was chosen to be Herbert Humphrey's running mate when Humphrey ran against Richard Nixon. The Humphrey-Muskie ticket lost by a mere .07 percent margin.

In 1972, Muskie was the frontrunner for the Democratic presidential nomination when his campaign was curtailed by a fake letter that later turned out to be

one of Nixon's dirty tricks—so he returned to the Senate. Jimmy Carter won the presidency in 1977, and in 1980 he tapped Muskie to be Secretary of State—the highest government office attained by a Polish-American. His term ended when Carter lost to Reagan in 1980.

Jimmy Carter awarded Muskie the Presidential Medal of Freedom in 1981. Years later, after his retirement from politics, Muskie was appointed to the "Tower Commission," the president's special review board that investigated the Reagan administration's role in the Iran-Contra affair.

Always a conservation-minded hunter and fisherman, Muskie had seen first-hand that Maine's great rivers were polluted by paper companies. In the Senate, he started working across the aisle to pass small bills to protect the environment. He has been called the most effective legislator of his generation.

> Many will remember Muskie primarily for his failed presidential run but it was his work in the Senate that was world-changing and provided a model for environmental protection.

As chair of the Subcommittee on Air and Water Pollution, Muskie in 1965 introduced a bill "to encourage prevention of pollution as well as to attack the problem and to find more efficient ways of doing it." He enlisted twenty-five co-sponsors and bipartisan support for his Water Quality Act directing states to develop water quality standards. Federal regulation was necessary since many water bodies crossed state lines. It passed and by the early '70s all states had developed and enacted water quality regulations which have been revised to reflect new scientific information.

Later he worked on air quality. Through his vision, persistence, attention to detail, willingness to work long hours, and do mounds of research, he chipped away at opposition until the Clean Air Act of 1970 passed Congress. Muskie was also a strong supporter of creating the Environmental Protection Agency, established in 1970.

When he died in 1996, Ed Muskie was eulogized by many, but particularly former President Jimmy Carter, who called him a "true statesman." Carter recalled that when he first became governor of Georgia, he faced nearly overwhelming lobbying pressure from power companies whose smokestacks were "spewing forth black smoke and the thirteen pulp mills in our state that were destroying our rivers . . . but there was a hero in Washington who faced much greater pressure nationwide from the polluters . . . Ed Muskie took them on and he inspired me and many others to do the same."

His contributions to clean air and water were not the only hallmarks of his Senate career. He also protected consumers through the 1970 Securities Investor Protection Act, insuring investors against the failures of brokerage houses, and the 1972 Truth-in-Government Act, which made government documents available to the public if their release didn't compromise national security. He wrangled the War Powers Act through the Senate in 1973, overturning Nixon's veto. It was the time of the Vietnam War, and though Muskie had supported it at the outset, by 1969 he had become outspoken in his criticism.

Once asked for comment on the direction the country was headed under Nixon, Muskie said, "In Maine we have a saying that there's no point in speaking unless you can improve on silence."

Muskie was also a champion of civil rights—having helped pass the landmark Civil Rights Act of 1964 that ended segregation. He helped pass federal aid to education, a national draft lottery, a lowering of the voting age to eighteen, and increases in Social Security benefits.

Muskie's papers are held at the Edmund S. Muskie Archives and Special Collections Library at Bates College in Lewiston. The University of Southern Maine has a public policy school named for him, The Muskie School of Public Service.

21

Uncle Tom's Cabin

HARRIET STOWE WAS BORN JUNE 14, 1811, IN LITCHFIELD, CONNECTICUT, THE SIXTH of eleven children born to the Reverend Lyman Beecher. Her mother died when Harriet was five and her father remarried. All seven of Lyman Beecher's sons became ministers, since the Stowes believed it was important to help shape the world and preaching was an effective way to accomplish this goal. The oldest daughter, Catherine, pioneered education for women. The youngest daughter, Isabella, helped found the National Women's Suffrage organization.

> "Never give up, for that is just the place and
> time the tide will turn."
> —*Harriet Beecher Stowe*

Harriet loved to write and started early, winning prizes in school when she was as young as seven. Her father encouraged and praised her writing. Her first published work was *Primary Geography for Children* in 1833, in which she shows an unusually sympathetic view of Catholicism for the time.

> "Women are the real architects of society."
> —*Harriet Beecher Stowe*

In 1832, when Harriet was twenty-one, her family moved to Cincinnati, where her father was appointed president of Lane Theological Seminary. There she met theology professor Calvin Stowe, who she described as "rich in Greek and Hebrew, Latin and Arabic, and alas! rich in nothing else . . ."

Flyer for a stage adaptation of *Uncle Tom's Cabin*.

They married and had seven children—one son died at eighteen months of cholera. Later, Stowe said the pain of her loss helped her understand the pain slave mothers felt when their children were taken and sold, lending inspiration for *Uncle Tom's Cabin*.

The book came about in part because in 1851 the publisher of *National Era* magazine asked Stowe to write a story about slavery to run in installments. He expected three or four installments, but Stowe wrote more than forty.

Publication of *Uncle Tom's Cabin* brought needed income to the family and enabled Stowe to spend her time writing. Over 51 years of writing, she published thirty books and innumerable short stories, poems, essays, magazine articles, and hymns. Two of her other books are the *Key to Uncle Tom's Cabin,* which documents case histories she used in her research, and *Dred: A Tale from the Swamp*, another anti-slavery novel, considered by many to be stronger than her first.

> "The bitterest tears shed over graves are for words left unsaid and deeds left undone."
>
> —*Harriet Beecher Stowe*

When Harriet Beecher Stowe met with Abraham Lincoln in Washington, D.C. after the Civil War had begun, the story goes that Lincoln said, "So you are the little woman who wrote the book that started this great war."

The Stowes moved to Andover, Massachusetts, for eleven years, then, when her husband retired, they moved to Hartford, Connecticut, where they remained, except for winters in Mandarin, Florida. Purchasing the Florida house served several goals besides a warmer winter for the family. The Stowes and the Beechers believed strongly in racial equality and social justice, and Charles Beecher—Harriet's brother—opened a school in Florida for emancipated slaves, asking his sister and her husband to join him.

In 2001, Bowdoin College bought the house at 63 Federal Street, in Brunswick, where Stowe had written her most famous book, and restored it. Known as The Harriet Beecher Stowe House, it is open to the public regularly and is a National Historic Landmark. The home, where she also sheltered South Carolina fugitive slave Andrew Jackson, was previously occupied by Henry Wadsworth Longfellow, when he was a Bowdoin student.

22

Joshua Chamberlain

THE OLDEST OF FIVE CHILDREN, JOSHUA LAWRENCE CHAMBERLAIN WAS BORN September 8, 1828, in Brewer, just eight years after Maine became a state. His father wanted him to join the military, his mother wanted him to be a preacher, but Chamberlain first chose to become an academic, even though he came from a long line of military men.

Chamberlain learned to read Ancient Greek and Latin in order to pass the entrance exam for Bowdoin College. He was chosen for the Phi Beta Kappa honor society and graduated in 1852.

He married, studied three more years at the Bangor Theological Seminary, then returned to Bowdoin as a professor of rhetoric. During his time on the faculty he taught every subject but science and math. He was fluent in nine languages, including Hebrew, Arabic, and Syriac.

When the Civil War broke out, Chamberlain believed all Northerners who were capable should fight for the Union, and preached this gospel in classes. Many Bowdoin faculty, however, did not share his enthusiasm for the war.

> Over the course of the Civil War, Chamberlain fought in twenty battles, had six horses shot out from under him, suffered six wounds, was cited for bravery four times, and was credited by some historians as having changed the course of the war.

Chamberlain wrangled a leave of absence, ostensibly to study languages in Europe. Instead, without informing his family or Bowdoin College, he enlisted in the Union Army and in 1862 was appointed Lieutenant Colonel of the 20th Maine Regiment.

The 20th fought valiantly at the Battle of Gettysburg in July of 1863, where Chamberlain's brigade was sent to defend a hill called Little Round Top. His men suffered many casualties and their position was charged repeatedly by a Confederate regiment. Then Chamberlain ordered a bayonet charge.

His men charged
down the hill, cap-
turing more than one
hundred Confederate
soldiers, and saving the
hill. For his "daring
heroism and tenacity,"
Chamberlain was award the Medal of Honor and came to be called "The Lion of the
Round Top."

In 1864, he was promoted and placed in charge of the 1st Brigade. That June,
Chamberlain and his men fought in the Second Battle of Petersburg, Virginia, where
he was shot through the right hip and groin. Chamberlain stuck his sword in the
ground to keep himself standing so his soldiers wouldn't retreat, but he soon collapsed
from blood loss and was so close to dying that his death was reported in Maine newspapers. He was given a deathbed promotion to brigadier general by Ulysses S. Grant.
Displaying his vaunted tenacity, however, Chamberlain recovered and returned to his
command in November.

By March 1865, he was in a major battle—variously known as Military Road,
Gravelly Run, or the Battle of Lewis's Farm—the start of a long siege that proved
a turning point in the war. Chamberlain again showed extreme courage. A bullet
went through his horse's neck, hit the frame of his wife's picture that he carried in

Chamberlain's Brunswick home, now the Joshua L. Chamberlain Museum, and home to the Pejepscot Historical Society.

his pocket, traveled through the skin of his chest along his rib, and exited through his back. All the soldiers thought he was shot right through the chest and marveled that he remained upright, encouraging them.

He nearly lost his left arm to the injury and was nearly captured, but the Union won the battle and he earned the nickname "Bloody Chamberlain." President Abraham Lincoln promoted him to major general. Chamberlain was selected a few weeks later to preside over the parade of Confederate soldiers for the formal surrender at Appomattox on April 12.

Returning to Maine as a conquering hero, Chamberlain was so popular he was elected governor, setting the record for the most votes for any governor. In the next election, he beat his own record. Altogether he ran and won four times.

When he quit politics, he returned to Bowdoin, was elected president of the college in 1871, and stayed until 1883, when his many war wounds caught up with him and he was forced to quit. Somehow, though, he managed to practice law in New York City, get involved in business ventures in Florida, New York, and the West Coast, volunteer but be rejected at age seventy for service in the Spanish-American War, and help found the Maine Institution for the Blind.

Finally, despite six operations to try to end a series of recurring infections caused by his war wounds, Chamberlain died in 1914 at age eighty-five in Portland. He was the last Civil War veteran to die from his war wounds, so he is considered the last Civil War casualty. His Brunswick home is now the Joshua L. Chamberlain Museum, where his original 1893 Medal of Honor is displayed. Chamberlain is buried in Pine Grove Cemetery in Brunswick.

23

Milton Bradley

MILTON BRADLEY—LITHOGRAPHER, BOARD GAME CREATOR, AND PROMOTER OF early childhood education—was born in Vienna, Maine, on November 8, 1836. He studied at the Lawrence Scientific School in Cambridge, Massachusetts, worked in a locomotive works in Springfield, then set up business as a mechanical draftsman and patent agent. In 1859 he studied lithography in Providence, Rhode Island, then returned to Springfield to set up the first color lithography shop, with the only lithograph machine in the state outside of Boston.

He established the Milton Bradley Company in 1860, when he was twenty-four, making lithographs on order for customers. He also printed an image of then scarcely-known Republican presidential candidate Abraham Lincoln. The lithographs sold briskly until Lincoln grew his distinctive beard and rendered them obsolete.

The Milton Bradley Company was the first successful manufacturer of board games in the U.S., and many of his games promoted positive childhood development. The company dominated the board game business throughout the 20th century. In addition to its flagship game, The Game of Life, Milton Bradley introduced many more successful games, such as Easy Money, Candy Land, Operation, Twister, and Battleship. The Game of Life was redesigned in the '60s and is now known simply as Life.

Milton Bradley is also considered one of the great 19th century American inventor-industrialists. He developed a lifelong interest in the work of Friedrich Froebel, a German who created the idea of kindergarten, or the "children's garden," to stimulate learning in small children through experience. Bradley is credited with helping launch the kindergarten movement in the U.S. He also manufactured educational games for students and introduced water color sets and crayon packages with standardized colors—before Crayola.

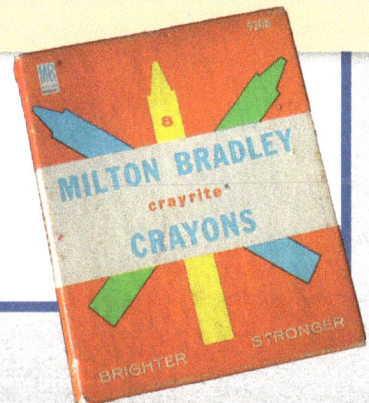

MILTON BRADLEY
crayrite
CRAYONS
BRIGHTER   STRONGER

In 1984, the company was purchased by the multinational, Rhode Island-based game and toy company, Hasbro. In 1991, Hasbro also purchased Parker Brothers, makers of Monopoly and other games, and once the biggest rival to Milton Bradley.

●●●

A business downturn prompted Bradley to pursue an idea he had simmering—a board game based on life itself. Most games of the period in Puritan New England were religious in nature, meant to edify and educate along Christian lines. Bradley decided his game would be secular, although still relying on moral virtues.

His "" was based on the squares of a checkerboard, and players used a numbered spinner because dice were considered representative of gambling and therefore immoral. The goal of the game was to advance from birth to a happy old age while avoiding financial ruin along the way. Squares on the board were good, bad, or neutral. Stopping on the "gambling" square sent the player back to "ruin" and landing on "intemperance" brought the player to "poverty." The first player to achieve 100 points won the game.

Bradley took a risk, printing up several hundred copies in the winter of 1860. In a two-day visit to New York he sold out his entire stock. By 1861, the game had sold an unheard-of 45,000 copies.

24

Louis Sockalexis

FIFTY YEARS BEFORE JACKIE ROBINSON BROKE THE COLOR BARRIER FOR AFRICAN Americans in baseball, Louis Sockalexis was the first Native American, and the first minority player, to play in the major leagues. He was a lightning-like pitcher, an amazing hitter, and an incredibly fast runner; plus he stole a lot of bases (six in one game). Sportswriter Harry Grayson said Sockalexis was faster than Ty Cobb, a better outfielder than Tris Speaker, and stronger than Babe Ruth.

> Former Yankees general manager Ed Barrow called Sockalexis "the best hitter, the best thrower, the best fielder, and also, the best drinker." This last 'best' was his downfall, unfortunately.

Louis Francis Sockalexis was born October 24, 1871, on Penobscot Indian Island Reservation, near Old Town, Maine. His father served as governor of the Penobscot Nation and his grandfather was Chief of the Bear Clan.

Louis grew to be muscular, nearly six feet tall, and was considered the best athlete in the tribe, winning all kinds of events from footraces to throwing contests. He loved baseball, and played with semi-pro teams around the state after high school. While playing for one of these, a teammate urged Sockalexis to enroll at the College of the Holy Cross in Worcester, Massachusetts.

At Holy Cross on scholarship, Sockalexis excelled at track and starred as a running back on the football team. But he broke records as a college baseball player, including the world record for the longest throw—138 feet. He stayed only two years at Holy Cross, batting over 400 each season. He is still ranked as one of the nine all-time greatest players for the school. He was being looked at by professional teams when he transferred to Notre Dame, where he stayed only a few months before being kicked out after brawling at a local bar.

> "I unhesitatingly pronounce him a wonder. Why he has not been snapped up before by some League club looking for a sensational player is beyond my comprehension."
> — *former Giants manager John Ward to* Sporting Life *magazine*

Sockalexis was recruited by the Cleveland major league team then known as the Spiders. When he showed up for training in 1897, Sockalexis wowed his teammates and coaches, and won the starting right field spot. After twenty games, his presence had increased attendance for two reasons: His novelty and reputation as a player attracted fans, but his ethnic derivation also attracted racists who hurled insults at the rookie. Sports writer Elmer Bates wrote that year, "He is hooted and bawled at by the thimble-brained brigade on the bleachers. Despite all this handicap the red man has played good, steady ball, and has been a factor in nearly every victory thus far won by Tebeau's team."

> In the early days, team names changed frequently. In 1897, local sportswriters began calling the Cleveland Spiders, "Tebeau's Indians," after manager Patsy Tebeau and Louis Sockalexis. The team later came to be known as the Naps, after a good player. It was not until 1914 that the team officially acquired the name Cleveland Indians, reportedly to honor Sockalexis.

Unfortunately, Sockalexis brought his drinking problem with him. Just months after joining the team, he got drunk and fell or jumped out of the second-story window of a brothel and sprained his ankle. Five days after the injury he returned to play, but was pulled from the game because he was visibly drunk and making errors. He appeared to clean up his act, and ended his first major league season with a .338 average and sixteen stolen bases.

The following year, he lost his starting position and spent a lot of time on the bench. In 1899, the Cleveland owner bought the St. Louis Browns but did not transfer Sockalexis to the Browns along with all of Cleveland's other star players. The Cleveland team went on to have the worst season in the history of major league baseball. Sockalexis relapsed during the season and barely played; when he did, he was so drunk he actually fell down on the field. He was released by the team and never played in the major leagues again.

After his release from the majors, Sockalexis had a mixed record with semi-pro teams until 1900. For two years he was reportedly homeless and often arrested for public drunkenness and disturbances and even spent some time in jail. In 1902, he

played a season in Lowell, Massachusetts, with a New England League team. The next year he briefly joined a Bangor team, which marked the end of his career in organized baseball.

When he returned to Indian Island, Sockalexis played for town teams, coached youngsters, ran a ferry boat, and went logging in the Maine woods. Although he may have stopped drinking, he was sick. On Christmas Eve of 1914, he suffered a massive heart attack while cutting down a large pine tree and died. He was 42.

Sockalexis played only 97 major league games during his short, intense career. The year he died, teammate Ed McKean paid homage to him: "He was a wild bird," said McKean. "He had more natural ability than any player I have ever seen, past or present."

In 2000, Sockalexis was voted into the American Indian Athletic Hall of Fame. During his career he was dubbed variously by sportswriters the "Deerfoot of the Diamond" and "Chief of Sockem." He was inducted into the Maine Sports Hall of Fame in 1985. Those wishing to honor him can visit his grave on Indian Island. In 1934, the state of Maine replaced the original wooden cross with a stone marker emblazoned with a baseball and crossed bats.

25

Peary and MacMillan

ROBERT EDWIN PEARY WAS THE FIRST PERSON CREDITED WITH REACHING THE North Pole with his expedition on April 6, 1909. His fellow Bowdoin College graduate, Donald Baxter MacMillan was on that expedition with Peary, but had to turn back due to injury before they reached the Pole. The pair, however, made many trips to the Arctic, together and separately.

Peary was born on May 6, 1856, in Pennsylvania. His father, Charles, died when he was three, and his mother, Mary, moved them to Portland, Maine. He attended Bowdoin, graduating with a civil engineering degree in 1877. After college, he moved to Washington, D.C. to work for the U.S. Coast and Geodetic Survey, then joined the Navy as a lieutenant stationed in the tropics.

> Apparently, Peary didn't like the heat—when he was in the Navy
> he was stationed in the tropics, and it was there that he decided
> he would be the first person to reach the North Pole.

He took six months' leave from the Navy in 1886 to make his first attempt to cross Greenland by dog sled, starting on the west coast. He and a companion stopped after 100 miles when their food supply ran low. He tried again in 1891, attempting a more difficult route. He made it about 1,250 miles and confirmed that Greenland is an island. In 1898 he made another expedition, achieving the distinction of reaching the "farthest north" of Ellesmere Island, Canada.

For his next expedition in 1905, Peary had a new ship built, the SS *Roosevelt,* and claimed another "farthest north by ship" record, as well as a "farthest north" without camping distinction. Peary made his final expedition in 1908, and claimed to have reached the North Pole on April 6, 1909. Upon his return to the U.S., the *New York Times* ran a story with the front-page headline: "Peary Discovers the North Pole After Eight Trials in 23 Years."

Left: Robert Peary on his 1909 Polar expedition. Right: Donald MacMillan in fur suit at wheel of ship *Bowdoin* ca. 1922.

With Peary on the expedition was Donald Baxter MacMillan. Peary had met Mac-Millan after MacMillan saved nine shipwrecked people. Unfortunately, MacMillan suffered from frozen heels and had to turn back 26 days before Peary reached the Pole.

After their return, Peary found that a former friend and shipmate claimed he had reached the Pole in April of 1908, a full year before Peary. A week before the *Times* story on Peary, the *New York Herald* ran a story with the headline, "The North Pole is Discovered by Dr. Frederick A. Cook." Cook had been a surgeon on the 1891–1892 Peary expedition.

The claims of Cook and Peary set off an argument among scientists
that is not fully resolved today, given that neither man could produce
definitive evidence that he had reached the Pole. Each claimed to have left
documents buried at the site of the Pole, but this evidence was never found.

Court trials supported Peary's claim and dismissed Cook's, so Congress commended Peary for having "attained," but not discovered, the Pole on March 3, 1911. In 1989, the National Geographic Society asked the Foundation for the Promotion of the Art of Navigation to investigate the issue. The Foundation concluded that Peary had reached the Pole and its president, Gilbert M. Grosvenor, said, "I consider this the end of a historic controversy and the confirmation of due justice to a great explorer."

On March 30, 1911, Peary was promoted to the rank of Rear Admiral and later that year, retired to Eagle Island, off Harpswell, Maine. His home there is a Maine State Historic Site. Peary died in Washington, D.C. on February 20, 1920, and is buried in Arlington National Cemetery.

MacMillan made more than thirty expeditions to the Arctic and pioneered the use of radios, airplanes, and electricity there. He established the MacMillan-Moravian School in 1929, took thousands of photographs of the Arctic, and published a dictionary of the Inuktitut language.

In 1913, MacMillan undertook an expedition to locate Crocker Land, a series of peaks Peary had spotted from a hill on the Greenland ice fields. It was assumed to be a new continent, but MacMillan's long ordeal —a two-year trip that turned into five years marked by blizzards, marooning, a murderous crewman, and a drunken captain— failed to turn up a continent.

MacMillan's last trip to the Arctic was in 1957 when he was 82 years old. He died at age 95 in Provincetown, Massachusetts.

Peary and MacMillan are honored by their alma mater, Bowdoin College, in Brunswick, Maine (Peary graduated Bowdoin in 1877 and MacMillan in 1898), with a museum named for their exploits. The Peary-MacMillan Arctic Museum is one of only two museums in the country dedicated to Arctic exploration.

MacMillan attended the opening of the museum in 1967. An Arctic Studies Center added in 1985 links the museum's resources. The library, with research and teaching efforts, hosts lectures, workshops, and educational outreach projects. Its exhibitions range from plants and animals to the cultural life of Arctic natives, and contain equipment used by Peary and MacMillan, as well as their papers, publications, and specimens.

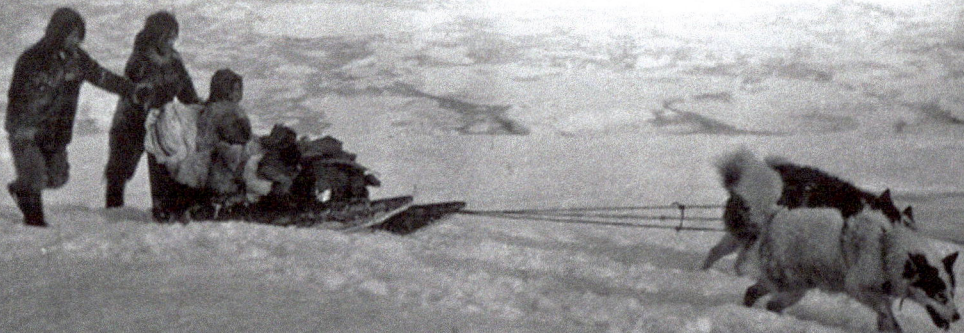

26

Telstar

ON JULY 11, 1962, IN THE FORMER LOGGING TOWN OF ANDOVER, MAINE, THE FIRST trans-Atlantic TV signal was relayed from a huge antenna, beamed to an experimental communications satellite called Telstar (which had only been launched the day before), and relayed back down to Europe. The new system allowed TV, faxes, and telephone calls to be broadcast live across the Atlantic Ocean for the first time. The two relay stations in Europe that received those first signals were located in northwestern France and southwestern England.

Besides marking the first trans-Atlantic transmission and an innovative satellite, the station itself was an engineering marvel. In order to construct the giant "horn" antenna, seven stories high and weighing 340 tons, engineers had to fabricate a temporary air-supported "radome" made of Dacron. When the antenna was completed, another, permanent radome was built to replace it that was 160 feet high and 210 feet wide.

Some corporations told the engineers their proposed materials and parts could not be built, however the hypothetical fabric, a composite of Hypalon and Dacron, was manufactured and worked. A special sealant was invented for the seams. It also worked. The radome had no structural support but was held up by tension and kept stable by air pressure alone and was described by some as a sixteen-story inflatable bubble.

Senator Margaret Chase Smith with a replica of the Telstar communications satellite, 1962.

"Our small company was going to build the largest radome ever conceived, using material that didn't exist, requiring joint strengths never achieved, using a new adhesive in a joint design still to be proved. All within a seemingly impossible time period."

—Milton B. Punnett, Telstar engineer

The location in Andover was chosen in December of 1960, land was purchased in January of 1961, and construction began May 1 with the target date for transmission in July of 1962. Equipment was installed in February 1962. Against all odds, this engineering marvel was ready for operation by spring.

The temporary radome was used to help place the permanent radome over the antenna. *Electronic Design* magazine called it "a giant equivalent to the magician's trick of removing someone's shirt without taking off their coat." Since both radomes were the same size, the new one had to be lowered by an attachment line, then floated over the old one using air and many cranes.

At 6:17 p.m. on July 11, 1962, President Lyndon Johnson and AT&T chairman Frederick Kappel held a telephone conversation relayed through Telstar. At 6:31, Andover sent out an image of the American flag in front of the Andover station, and the French station received the image at 6:45, and the English station received it at 7:00 p.m.

In 1962, all Maine telephone books featured a drawing of the Andover station on their covers. In 1968, the new high school in Bethel was named Telstar in honor of the communications breakthrough. During the 1960s, some 25,000 people a year visited the facility.

But modern technology is a fleeting thing, and satellite communications technology changed. Andover's radome was dismantled in the 1990s, but in France and England the radomes were retained and designated as historic sites.

During the winter of 1961-'62, the heat in the dome failed at one point during construction. Being winter in Maine a large amount of snow accumulated atop the dome. When the heat was restored, the snow melted and formed a lake on top. The workers decided the best way to get rid of the water was to shoot a hole in the dome. As the pressure equalized, the ice and water were thrown off, but a large piece of ice fell on a work trailer and crushed it.

Senator Margaret Chase Smith in August 1962
gesturing to a large photograph of the Telstar
earth station in Andover, Maine.

Bell Laboratories in New Jersey produced
the Telstar satellite and built the Andover
station. Bell considered locating the station in New Jersey, but Maine was chosen
because of geography. Maine is closer to
Europe, and the Andover site allowed the
antenna to be sited in a bowl, surrounded by
mountains, where practically no microwave
interference would occur.

27

Bridge in a backpack

IT SOUNDS LIKE A KID'S TOY OR PERHAPS A JOKE, BUT THE "BRIDGE-IN-A-BACKPACK" is the real deal with the potential to revolutionize bridge building the world over. Invented and designed at the University of Maine, Orono's Advanced Structures and Composites Center, the Bridge-in-a-Backpack reduces construction time, lowers costs, and can double the life span of bridges.

Using new technology, lightweight tubes that will form arches for a bridge are constructed in Orono, delivered by truck to a site in bags that resemble big sports duffles, then inflated at the site and imbued with resin.

The inflated arches are then filled with concrete on the spot where they will be used— reducing the cost of transportation and the carbon footprint while using fewer people and less heavy equipment. Instead of months, bridges can be constructed in days or weeks.

After the arches are filled with concrete and set in the river, crews lay a deck across the top. It has been called a "rapidly deployable bridge for military purposes," although the first round of bridges were built for communities.

Their ease and speed of building does not mean they are only temporary fixes— the bridges are strong enough to last at least a hundred years and require no maintenance. Since the tubes are made of impervious composite and the concrete is inside, protected by the tube, engineers say there is nothing used in the construction that can corrode. There is no steel rebar to rust and the composite creates a barrier to protect against road salt, chemicals, and moisture.

Bridge-in-a-Backpack technology has been used to construct spans in Maine, New Hampshire, Vermont, and Michigan; as well as the first international bridge, a 26-foot span in Trinidad.

Founded in 1996, the composites center has grown rapidly in two decades— expanding staff and adding buildings for additional labs and offices. Besides bridges, the technology has applications for defense and aerospace, other forms of infrastructure, and ocean energy.

The spin-off private company, Advanced Infrastructure Technology—which mostly employs UMaine engineering graduates who worked at the composites center—was formed in 2008 and licensed to design and construct the bridges.

In 2007, the American Composites Manufacturers Association (ACMA) presented their People's Choice Award to the Bridge-in-a-Backpack for innovation and creativity. The bridge was also awarded the Most Creative Product Award by the ACMA in 2010; the Engineering Excellence Award by the American Council of Engineering Companies in 2011, and the Charles Pankow Award for Innovation by the American Society of Civil Engineers in 2011.

Professor Habib Dagher, a founding director of UMaine Advanced Structures and Composites Center was recognized by the White House and presented with an award in 2015 commending him as a Transportation Champion of Change. Dagher is included on 24 patents with eight more pending.

These lightweight, efficient arches are designed and constructed for each specific small- to medium-sized bridge. The system may be used to provide quick fixes in war-torn areas throughout the world, where old bridges have been destroyed or new ones are needed to transport supplies. They are also efficient for rebuilding after major weather events, or for merely replacing crumbling infrastructure.

28

Maine Coon Cat

MAINE COON CATS HAVE BEEN AROUND SINCE COLONIAL DAYS, ALTHOUGH THEIR TRUE origins are murky at best. The first cat called by the name appears in cat literature from 1861, a black and white named "Captain Jenks of the Horse Marines."

This largest of domestic breeds grows more slowly than other cats, usually not reaching its full size until they are three to five years old. The "Longest Cat" was a Maine coon recorded in 2010 by the Guinness Book of World records. Stewie, of Reno, Nevada, measured 48.5 inches from the tip of his nose to the tip of his tail—the average domestic cat measures 18 inches.

Coon cats are considered native to Maine and were adopted as the official Maine State Cat in 1985.

Like dogs, Maine Coon cats are trainable (for instance, to be walked on a leash), playful, loyal to their family, tend to follow their owners around, and are cautious, but not unfriendly, with strangers. They are known to get on well with dogs, other cats, and children. Since they are so large, people are often surprised by some of the softer sounds coon cats make, such as cheeping, trilling, or chirping. But they are vocal by nature and capable of much louder howl

Stewie's title was passed on in 2016 (Stewie died in 2013) to another Maine coon named Ludo from Wakefield, England, who is five centimeters shorter than Stewie. Ludo's owner was inspired to get one after seeing a Maine coon cat in the Harry Potter films.

Male coon cats weigh on average from 13 to 18 pounds, and females usually between 8 and 12 pounds, but they can reach 20 pounds or more. They are highly intelligent with muscular bodies and broad chests.

Their huge paws are useful for walking on snow without breaking through, and the long tufts of fur that grow between their toes help keep their paws warm. The tufts of fur inside their ears do the same thing. Their thick coat repels water and their tails can be used as a warm seat when they sit

on ice, or may be curled around their face when lying in windy or snowy places—all characteristics the breed developed to adapt to harsh winter conditions.

There is no shortage of myths about the origin of the coon cat, including claims the breed originated as the result of domestic cats mating with either raccoons or bobcats. However, these myths are just that, since it is biologically impossible for cats to mate with either creature.

Still another legend says six of Marie Antoinette's Turkish Angora cats were sent to the New World along with her prized possessions ahead of her intended escape during the French Revolution. When she was executed, those cats were released in Wiscasset to breed with local cats. However, six cats are hardly enough to produce a new breed, and long-haired cats had already been brought to Maine by other ships.

Others say the local shorthairs mated with longhairs brought by the Vikings on their travels between Iceland, Greenland, Newfoundland—and possibly, Boston and the coast of Maine. While there is no proof the Vikings brought cats, the Maine coon does most closely resemble the Norwegian Forest Cat, or Skogkatt, a naturally occurring breed from Scandinavia. Lending a bit more credence to this theory, one author said DNA connects some cats from Iceland and cats where Vikings may have visited.

Like Maine coon cats, Skogcatts—which came out of the woods and became domesticated within the last few thousand years—are friendly and like people. A lot of coon cats seem to have a fascination with water, which some experts say could have derived from ancestors who spent a lot of time at sea.

In the early 20th century, the coon cat was an extremely popular breed, but more exotic breeds were introduced and gradually the coon cat's popularity waned, and the breed nearly disappeared by the 1950s.

However, breeders founded an association to prevent the demise of the coon cat, held shows just for the breed, and finally were allowed to show at all-breed competitions again. By 1980, the breed was recognized by all registries. Now the Maine Coon cat is the third most popular breed in the country.

29

The Whoopie Pie

THE WHOOPIE PIE IS NOT A PIE AT ALL, BUT A SINFULLY DELICIOUS SWEET CONSISTING of two soft, small, mounded cakes (sometimes called "cookies" or "shells") with a delicious sweet filling sandwiched between them. These days, the cakes and fillings may be flavored with nearly anything, but the originals were dark chocolate cakes with white vanilla filling.

Even traditionalists will argue the content of the "authentic" filling or the proper recipe for the cakes. But most agree that the cakes should be a devils food-like dark chocolate. Agreement on the correct filling is more difficult to reach.

There are those who say the filling must contain some Marshmallow Fluff, a product from Massachusetts rarely found outside New England. Others insist the filling should have raw, whipped egg whites paired with vegetable shortening and sugar (these must be refrigerated), while others opt for butter to make a filling that more strongly resembles buttercream frosting.

Maine has the first shop devoted entirely to the whoopie pie, which was opened by the same woman who holds the record for the World's Largest Whoopie Pie. In 2011, Amy Bouchard of Isamax Snacks constructed a 1,067-pound whoopie pie that required a tractor trailer to deliver it and a forklift to put the layers in place.

In Maine (and Pennsylvania), most everyone remembers the whoopie pies their grandmothers and mothers made, and often use the same recipe handed down for generations. Each state claims it invented the whoopie pie.

A bakery in Lewiston, Maine, claims to have made them since 1925, but a fire destroyed the bakery's records in 1967, so the claim can't be proven. Pennsylvania claims the Amish created them. Food historians also point to ads for whoopie pies from a Boston commercial bakery that appeared in newspapers in the early 1930s.

Since no one can prove where the whoopie pie originated, the state of Maine, which produces many millions of them annually, adopted the whoopie pie as its

Official State Treat in 2011. The whoopie pie can be found for sale in convenience stores and supermarkets, and as dessert in restaurants of all types.

Whoopie pies are baked throughout the state in tiny gourmet bakeries, café bakeries devoted to them, and in giant commercial bakeries that supply supermarkets and other private label outfits around the country and the world with millions of the desserts. When the fame of whoopie pies took off outside its traditional area around 2010, love of the confection reached not only across the country, but around the world, from London and Paris to as far away as Dubai.

30

The Washburn Brothers

"The Washburns left a record of achievement that will probably never be equaled again by a single generation of any American family."
—*Kerck Kelsey*

ALTHOUGH THEY LIVED IN POVERTY AND ENJOYED ALMOST NO ADVANTAGES, ALL seven sons of Israel Washburn and his wife, Martha Benjamin, attained remarkable achievements. Four were elected and re-elected to Congress. Two were considered as Republican candidates for president and vice president. Two were elected state governors—one in Maine during the Civil War. Two were ambassadors. One was a Civil War general. One a Civil War Navy captain. One founded a railroad. One owned a bank. One ran a newspaper. Two established great flour mills that ended up as the giant General Mills.

And yet, despite their accomplishments as state, national, and international politicians, military men, diplomats, inventors, and businessmen, the Washburn names are not household words. Their mother is largely credited with instilling their ambition to succeed.

The first to make money was the second child, Algernon Sidney "Sid" Washburn (1814–1879.) Sid left home at age fifteen, owned a store in Boston, moved back home and became co-founder of a Hallowell bank, then later organized the First National Bank of Hallowell. Sid shared the wealth by making loans to his younger brothers when needed. They always paid him back.

Israel Washburn Jr.

First-born was Israel Washburn Jr. (1813–1887), who became a lawyer in 1834 and was elected to the Maine House of Representatives in 1842, Congress in 1851, and governor of Maine in 1861 and 1862. He was the most influential of the brothers in helping form the Republican Party. He was appointed a collector for the port of Portland by President Lincoln, and was later president of the Rumford Falls Railroad.

The Washburn-Norlands estate, or the Washburn-Norlands Living History Center, has four historic buildings, including the 1867 Gothic-Revival mansion, the 1883 library, the 1828 Meeting House and the 1853 school house. Each is restored and operates as a museum and repository of collections, including Washburn family papers, photographs, artwork, historic clothing, books, and furniture. This 19th-century homestead, the center of so much important history, is on the National Register of Historical Places and functions as a living history museum regularly visited by schoolchildren.

Elihu Benjamin Washburne (1816–1887) added the ancestral "e" to the end of his surname. He left at age thirteen to work on a neighbor's farm to pay off a debt of his father's, (as did all four older sons.) He went on to become a lawyer and moved to Galena, Illinois. Elected to the U.S. House of Representative in 1852, he stayed there until 1869, earning the nicknames "Father of the House" and "Watchdog of the Treasury." After Congress he moved to Paris for eight years as U.S. Minister to France, where he was the only foreign minister to stay after the siege of Paris during the Franco-Prussian War, and "the Commune" period to protect all foreigners abandoned by their ministers. He was personal friends with Lincoln and Ulysses Grant.

He returned to Chicago to engage in literary pursuits before his death in 1887 and interment in Galena.

Cadwallader "Cad" Colden Washburn (1818–1882) came next. The first to move west in 1842, he practiced law in Mineral Point, Wisconsin, owned a land office and bank and later made a fortune in lumbering, saw mills, and flour. Two brothers were already serving in Congress when he was elected in 1855. He left to become a Civil War major general, returned to Congress after the war for two terms, and was later elected governor of Wisconsin. His flour company won bronze, silver, and gold in the Miller's International Exhibition in Cincinnati, Ohio, in 1880, and was later dubbed Gold Medal Flour.

Charles Ames Washburn (1822–1889) was the next success story. A graduate of Kents Hill Wesleyan Seminary and Bowdoin College, he headed to California, where he achieved success in the Gold Rush. His gold financed a career as writer and editor of a newspaper in San Francisco. He served as U.S. Minister to Paraguay from 1861 to 1868, where he offered to mediate between the allies and Paraguay during the "War of the Triple Alliance." When things turned sour, Charles proclaimed himself protector of all foreign residents in Asuncion, was declared a spy, and had to be rescued from his post by a U.S. warship. He also held a patent on Washburn's Typeograph, an important typewriter element, which he sold to the Remington Company. He also wrote a two-volume history of Paraguay.

Cadwallader Washburn.

William Drew Washburn (1831–1912) also graduated from Bowdoin College, studied law with brother Israel, and eventually settled in Minnesota, where he built dams and flour- and saw- mills. His flour mill eventually merged with the Pillsbury Flour Company. He became a congressman and later a senator, and founded the SOO Railroad.

Samuel Benjamin Washburn (1824-1890) was the only one who went to sea, at the age of eighteen. During the Civil War he was Acting Master in the Navy and an officer of the gunboat *Galena*. A hip wound during a gun battle left him lame. He returned home in 1871 to care for his aging father in Livermore.

Henry Wadsworth Longfellow

HENRY WADSWORTH LONGFELLOW IS A WELL-KNOWN AMERICAN POET WHOSE RHYMING, story-telling poems are studied by most U.S. students at some point in their education.

Born in Portland, Maine, in 1807, he was one of eight children of Stephen and Zilpah (Wadsworth) Longfellow. Longfellow showed his literary tendencies early, anonymously contributing a poem to the *Portland Gazette* in 1820 when he was only thirteen.

Longfellow's home, ca. 1900.

He was raised in a home built by Zilpah's father, Peleg Wadsworth, at 489 Congress Street, now a National Historic Landmark known as the Wadsworth-Longfellow House. He was educated at Portland Academy, where he became fluent in Latin, a harbinger of his future interest and fluency in European languages.

Young Henry was greatly affected by the War of 1812, which not only devastated the Portland economy, but brought the horrors of war close to home. His poem "My Lost Youth" recalls a naval battle of 1813 between a British ship, *Boxer*, and the American *Enterprise*. The Americans won, but both young captains died and were interred in the Eastern Cemetery near Henry's house.

At the age of fifteen, Henry enrolled at Maine's first college, Bowdoin, which their grandfather helped found and of which their father was a trustee. He graduated in 1825, along with famed author Nathaniel Hawthorne, who remained a lifelong friend.

His father wished Henry to study law, but the boy knew his true calling was literature, telling his father, "my whole soul burns most ardently after it…"

In 1829, he joined the faculty of Bowdoin, teaching French, Spanish, and Italian. He married Mary Potter, began writing critical essays and published six language texts. On a fateful trip to Europe in 1835, Mary died in childbirth. Although in a deep

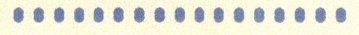

Longfellow was not only able to support himself and his family by his writing, but he became one of the biggest international best-selling authors. For seven years he and his family lived an idyllic family life, enjoyed material comfort and the company of the leading literary lights of the age—including Hawthorne, Emerson, and Oliver Wendell Holmes.

depression, Longfellow soldiered on. He also met his future wife in the Alps, though Frances "Fanny" Appleton resisted his advances for the next seven years.

Longfellow began teaching at Harvard in 1836 and also launched his literary career with the autobiographical novel *Hyperion* and two poetry collections, *Voices in the Night* and *Ballads and Poems*. These works were immediate sensations in the U.S. and Europe, and by 1843, Fanny agreed to marry him. The home where the Longfellows raised their six children in Cambridge was given to the couple by her father as a wedding gift. It was already famous as the headquarters for George Washington during the Siege of Boston from July 1775 to April 1776. It is now the Longfellow House–Washington's Headquarters National Historic Site.

His fame continued with his *Poems on Slavery, Evangeline: A Tale of Acadie, Kavanagh, The Song of Hiawatha*, and *The Courtship of Miles Standish*. By 1854, he was such a literary success, he was able to leave Harvard. Longfellow was described as having a gentle, sweet personality. He also received high payment for his work, sums unheard of in the day. By 1874, he was receiving $3,000 per poem.

His poem "Evangeline," about lovers separated during the expulsion of the Acadians from Nova Scotia, was one of the most famous of his works. It has inspired movies, songs, and a statue in Grand-Pré, Nova Scotia, along with a reconstruction of a French church. His version of the Acadian expulsion, exclusively blaming the British, has been challenged by later historians, but there is no doubt he rightfully upset the accepted view that the British founded Nova Scotia, by illuminating the 150-year history of the Acadians who were there before the British founded Halifax. Within ten years of its publication, Evangeline had sold 36,000 copies.

Then tragedy struck again. Fanny was melting sealing wax in 1861 when her clothing burst into flames. Longfellow tried to put the fire out and sustained burns on his face and hands. Fanny died the next day. Most pictures of Longfellow show him wearing a full beard, the beard he grew to cover the scars from his burns. He continued to write, but his best poems were behind him, and he concentrated on the translation of other works.

Longfellow was easily the most popular poet of his day. The occasion of his 70th birthday was treated as a national holiday, with parades, readings, and speeches. Although some critics assailed his work as imitative of European styles, many of his contemporaries admired his work greatly. Hawthorne once wrote to him: "I read your poems over and over . . . nothing equal to some of them was ever written in this world."

84

32

Penobscot Narrows Bridge

THE PENOBSCOT NARROWS OBSERVATORY, WITH ALL ITS ENGINEERING FIRSTS, IS at the forefront of bridge design throughout the world. The bridge connects the town of Prospect to Verona Island on Route 1 and has the first bridge observatory in the country—and at 420 feet (taller than the Statue of Liberty), it's the tallest one in the world.

With an award-winning, innovative design, the observatory offers a 360-degree view of the Penobscot River and surrounding Penobscot Bay, river, woods, islands, mountains, and fields. On a clear day, the 100-mile radius of visibility means visitors may see Mount Katahdin, Cadillac Mountain, and the Camden Hills all from the 13-by-25-foot observation room. Plaques under each of four glass walls show the compass points and maps of the view.

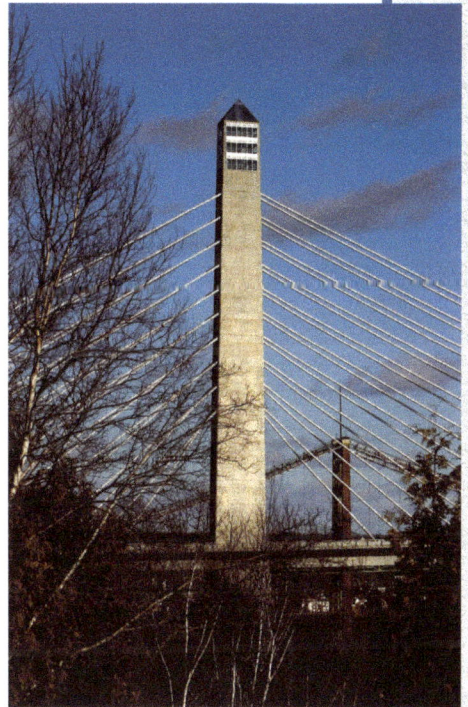

The observatory itself is shaped like the Washington Monument and comprises one of the two major supports for the 2,120-foot cable-stayed bridge that replaced the old Waldo-Hancock bridge in 2007. The fastest elevator in Northern New England wings visitors skyward 400 feet in less than a minute, then there's a climb of around three dozen steps to the top.

Along with the sweeping overland vistas, the view of the Penobscot River running through a steep gorge directly below the observatory is impressive. When it opened in 2007, the observatory became the most popular attraction in mid-coast Maine almost immediately.

The bridge's base is made from slabs of granite, an homage to Maine's granite industry, and granite steps lead to the parking area.

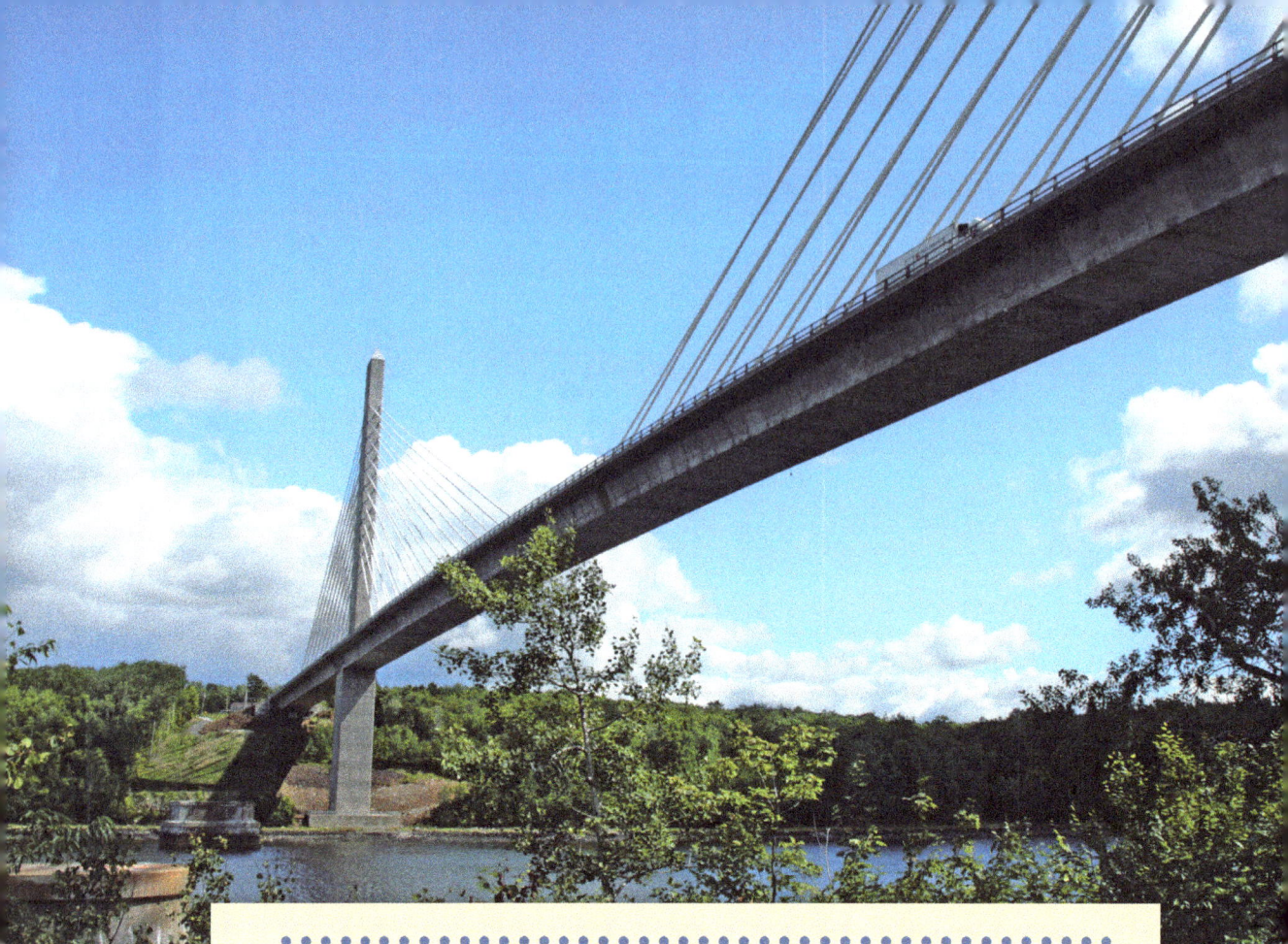

A MODERN MARVEL

The bridge has been called one of the most impressive engineering structures in the world. One of only two bridges in the U.S. that employs a cradle system, meaning the cable strands are carried from the bridge deck within long white tubes called stays, eliminating the need to anchor the cables in the pylons.

Epoxy-coated steel inside a 1-inch tube makes up the cables, an innovate design that allows individual strands to be inspected, then removed and replaced if necessary, while other cable bridges require removing entire groups of cables at once. Super-pressurized nitrogen gasses are used in the cable-stay system to help prevent corrosion.

Another first for the bridge is the testing of carbon fiber strands. Six have been inserted with the other cables and, because of the innovative use of separate strands, they can be monitored regularly. They are expected to prove stronger and longer-lasting than the steel strands.

33

Joan Benoit Samuelson

JOAN BENOIT SAMUELSON WAS BORN MAY 16, 1957, IN CAPE ELIZABETH, THE THIRD of four children born to Nancy and Andre Benoit. Both parents were skiers and encouraged athleticism in their children.

"Joanie," the only name Benoit needs in Maine, attended public school in Cape Elizabeth and was always athletic, but she did not start running until high school, after she broke her leg skiing when she hit a slalom gate. To help recover from the injury, she began to focus on track and field hockey.

She moved on to Bowdoin College, but in 1977, after two years at Bowdoin, she accepted a running scholarship to North Carolina State. In 1977 and 1978 she earned All-America honors and helped lead the school to a cross-country championship in the Atlantic Coast Conference.

> She is now Maine's most recognizable athlete, but before Benoit was a pioneer for women's running, she was a virtual unknown, until she won the Boston Marathon.

Benoit returned to Bowdoin to complete her degree in history and environmental studies, and in 1979 she entered the Boston Marathon. One of the oldest marathons in the country, run continuously since 1897, the race had banned women until 1972. She won with a time of 2:35:15, nearly eight minutes below the record.

That was just the beginning. She was set to compete in the 1980 Olympics until the United States boycotted the Moscow event. She ran, won, and set records in a few half-marathons before placing third in the Boston Marathon in 1981. Her rigorous race schedule caused many injuries and she required tendon and foot surgery for bone spurs, scar tissue, and other issues. Benoit feared she might never run again, but instead she recovered and was breaking records again by 1982 in several shorter races and one marathon in Oregon.

After winning the Boston Marathon in 1983, Joan Benoit Samuelson was training heavily for the Olympics, but she injured her knee during a 20-mile run and had arthroscopic knee surgery just seventeen days before the U.S. Olympic trials. A quick recovery led her to victory in the trials, and again in the Los Angeles Olympics, where she bested legendary runners Grete Waitz, Rosa Mota, and Ingrid Kristiansen in the first ever Olympics women's marathon.

The diminutive Samuelson—five-foot-one and barely 100 pounds—went on to win the Boston Marathon again in 1983, setting a world record of 2:22:43 that would not be broken for eleven years. She placed first in the trials for the first Olympic Women's Marathon in 1984, then won the marathon itself, setting an Olympic record of 2:24:52 and beating her nearest competitor by a minute and a half.

Besides winning Olympic gold, 1984 was a banner year for Benoit. She won the Jessie Owens Award, was named the Women's Sports Foundation Amateur Sportswoman of the year, and married her husband, Scott Samuelson. They have two children, a daughter, Abby, and a son, Anders.

The next year she won the 1985 Chicago marathon, setting an American record of 2:21:21 that held for eighteen years. Also in 1985, she won the James E. Sullivan Award for the best amateur athlete in the United States. She has run marathons as far away as New Zealand, but still runs in smaller races in Maine as well.

She allegedly retired, but continues to run, usually winning her age group in Boston, Chicago, and New York marathons. In 1998, she founded the Beach to Beacon 10K Road Race in her hometown of Cape Elizabeth. Winners have come from all over the world and registration usually fills up in less than two hours.

In 2014, she ran the Boston Marathon with both of her children. In 2012, she did not win her class in Boston because she chose to run the entire race with her daughter. She was inducted into the Maine Women's Hall of Fame in 2000.

After winning the Boston Marathon in 1983, Joan Benoit Samuelson was training heavily for the Olympics, but she injured her knee during a 20-mile run and had arthroscopic knee surgery just seventeen days before the U.S. Olympic trials. A quick recovery led her to victory in the trials, and again in the Los Angeles Olympics, where she bested legendary runners Grete Waitz, Rosa Mota, and Ingrid Kristiansen in the first ever Olympics women's marathon.

34

Elijah Parish Lovejoy

BORN NOVEMBER 9, 1802 IN ALBION, ELIJAH PARISH LOVEJOY WAS NAMED FOR ENGLISH cleric Elijah Parish, a friend of his father, who was a congregational minister. Educated at home in the Christian faith and in Maine's public schools, Lovejoy went on to Waterville College (now Colby College) in 1823. He was bright and athletic, and upon graduation in 1826, became a public school teacher in nearby China.

Finding the job to be not challenging enough, Elijah packed up and moved to the new state of Illinois seeking fresh experiences. Finding insufficient challenges, he went on to St. Louis, Missouri, where for a time he taught at school. But he tired of teaching, bought a half interest in the *St. Louis Times* newspaper, and became its editor.

Later, in 1831, a time of great religious revival in the country, he decided to study for the Presbyterian ministry at Princeton Theological Seminary. Upon receiving his preacher's license in 1833, he returned to St. Louis as pastor of the Des Peres Presbyterian Church and to edit *The Observer,* a Presbyterian weekly. He consistently wrote editorials opposing slavery and calling for abolition, but many readers in this slave state protested even his proposals for ending slavery gradually.

According to John Quincy Adams, Lovejoy was "the first American martyr to the freedom of the press and the freedom of the slave." Although his name is little known today, some credit Lovejoy's death and John Brown's raid on Harper's Ferry as the two most important events leading to the onset of the Civil War. Some even consider his death to be the first battle of the Civil War

The anger of the pro-slavery people increased with the prospect of slave revolts. In 1835, a group of citizens warned him to stop writing his anti-slavery editorials. He did not stop and continued to argue in print for freedom of the press, freedom of speech, and against slavery. In 1836 he wrote an account of the brutal burning of black freeman Francis Macintosh in St. Louis and of the trial that acquitted the leaders of the lynch mob.

Lovejoy's account of the brutal burning incited another mob, one that burglarized his home and burned his press. He moved to Alton, Illinois, a free state across the river, figuring he might successfully write there without repercussions. Alton was in a free state, but it was also a center for slave catchers trying to intercept slaves who crossed the Mississippi to freedom. When Lovejoy's press was shipped to Alton, a mob met it at the dock and smashed it.

He expected to write less about slavery in Illinois, but he told a gathering of citizens concerned about his anti-slavery stance, "as long as I am an American citizen, and as long as American blood runs in these veins, I shall hold myself at liberty to speak, to write, and to publish whatever I please on any subject."

A group of local citizens raised money to buy him another press and Lovejoy managed to publish for a year without incident. But in July of 1867, he wrote a strongly-worded editorial condemning slavery and a mob destroyed his press that night. Lovejoy persisted, however, bought another press, which was again destroyed. This time, his friends organized a militia when they bought another press.

The militia was there when a mob attacked the new press on the night of November 7, 1837. Although the militia fought bravely and killed one member of the mob, the mob torched the building, driving out the militia. When Lovejoy attempted to put out the fire, a mob member shot and killed him. He was buried on his 35th birthday, November 9, 1837.

> Since 1952, Lovejoy has been honored annually in Maine by his alma mater, Colby College, which presents the Elijah Parish Lovejoy Award to a newspaper reporter, editor, or publisher who exemplifies his courage in the practice of their profession. In 2000, Lovejoy was inducted into the Maine Press Hall of Fame.

Engraving of the burning of the warehouse and death of Lovejoy on November 7, 1837.

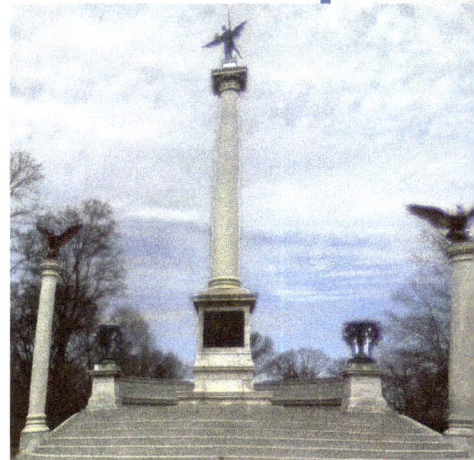

The 110-foot tall Elijah P. Lovejoy monument, in Alton, Illinois.

35

Molly Spotted Elk

MOLLY SPOTTED ELK WAS BORN MOLLY DELLIS NELSON ON THE PENOBSCOT Nation's Indian Island, near Old Town, on November 17, 1903 to basket maker Philomena Solis Nelson and Horace Nelson. Her father was the first Penobscot to go to Dartmouth College and he later became a governor-chief of the Penobscot Nation.

While the family ranked high in the Penobscot Nation—her grandfathers on both sides had been tribal leaders and her sister, Eunice, was the first Penobscot to earn a PhD.—they were still poor. She cleaned houses to pay for ballet lessons in Bangor, then worked her way through two years at the University of Pennsylvania by scrubbing floors. She studied anthropology and while there contributed to a book written by professor Frank Speck called *Penobscot Man.*

In 1930, Molly Spotted Elk appeared in the silent movie *The Silent Enemy* as Neewa, daughter of the tribal chief. The Silent Enemy of the title is hunger. As the tribe's food runs out, the chief must take advice from either of two men, both of whom wish to marry his daughter.

Filmed in Ontario and billed as a documentary about Indians in Northern Canada, the film was released in the U.S. and Canada, all over Europe, and in South America. It was first appearance of a Penobscot in a movie and the film contained one of the first zoom lens shots. It was one of the last silent films made by Paramount and was not a success. Lost for forty years, the film resurfaced and is now available for viewing at Indian Island and is used in anthropology classes at college

She had entered and won a Native American dance contest in Oklahoma and was "adopted" by the Cheyenne and given the name Spotted Elk, so when touring, she called herself Molly Spotted Elk.

When she was only thirteen, she had helped support her family by performing native dances, so when her money ran out at university, she took to the road performing native dance in vaudeville houses with the legendary Texas Guinan troupe.

She wrote her own music, made her own costumes, and enchanted audiences all across the country. While in New York City, she did many things to earn money to send home, including modeling nude for Greenwich Village artists, modeling footwear, and giving dance lessons.

Molly sailed for Europe in 1931 as a member of the ballet troupe of the International Colonial Exposition, representing American Indians. After fulfilling her commitment, she set out across Europe, entertaining audiences that included the likes of King Alphonso of Spain.

She returned to the U.S. briefly, appearing as an extra in a few Hollywood films, but returned to Europe in 1937 and settled in Paris, where she studied at the Sorbonne, researched Penobscot contact with the French, taught dance, and met a journalist named John Stephen Frederic Archambaud.

They married, but he lost his job during the Depression. She returned to the U.S., found some work, gave birth to their daughter, Jean, and returned to Paris in 1938, where she wrote a book of Penobscot stories. They were separated again by World War II. Molly fled France, crossing the Pyrenees on foot with her daughter, and returned to the U.S. She never saw her husband again, although she continued to try to find out what became of him.

Toward the end of her life, Molly wrote for long hours, pounding out children's stories. She left behind a book of traditional Penobscot stories in English, *Katahdin: Wigwam's Tales of the Abnaki Tribe* and a *Dictionary of Penobscot Passamaquoddy Words*.

She also crafted traditional dolls, two of which are in the Smithsonian. Molly died on Indian Island, on February 21, 1977 at the age of 73.

Although she was the toast of the U.S. vaudeville circuit and Europe's music halls, Molly Spotted Elk was always torn between home and her city life among artists and creative people, even though her performing career meant acting out stereotypes to meet the expectations of white audiences. Her biographer, Bunny McBride, wrote that Molly's return to Maine after New York and Paris "was like an old pair of moccasins that one dreamed of during years of high-heeled city life—only to find, upon slipping into them, that they felt less comfortable than remembered because the shape of one's feet had changed."

36

The Zig-Zag Stitch

IN AN ERA WHERE WOMEN WERE RARELY, IF EVER, EDUCATED AS ENGINEERS, HELEN Augusta Blanchard secured many patents for engineering changes to sewing machines that revolutionized the sewing industry, all without benefit of any training.

Born in Portland, on October 25, 1840, Blanchard was one of six children of a wealthy ship-owner and businessman. Unfortunately, her father lost his money and the family homestead in the panic of 1866. He died soon after, leaving the family in financial difficulty.

Helen apparently showed an inventive side at an early age, but never worked to achieve a patentable invention until after her father died. She moved to Boston and received her first patent in 1873 for a zig-zag, or buttonhole, stitch.

She moved to Philadelphia where she founded the Blanchard Overseaming Company in order to market her inventions in the 1870s. In 1882, she founded the Blanchard Hosiery Machine Company. Blanchard moved to New York in the early 1890s and continued to patent inventions, including a pencil sharpener and an improved surgical needle. In 1893, she was featured in an encyclopedia of prominent women.

The zig-zag stitch accomplished many things, including a way to close a seam and give the piece more strength, plus it made the job of seamstresses sewing buttonholes easier and quicker. She also invented the Blanchard over-seaming machine, which trimmed and sewed a seam simultaneously on knitted fabrics.

Blanchard profited sufficiently from her businesses and patents to buy back the family homestead in Portland. She moved back to Maine in 1901, continuing to patent inventions until 1916, when she had a stroke. She died in Providence, Rhode Island, in 1922, at age 82, but is buried in her family's plot in Evergreen Cemetery in Portland.

Helen Blanchard was inducted into the National Inventors Hall of Fame in 2006. An original 1873 zig-zag machine is displayed at the Museum of American History in Washington, D.C. While the names of Singer and Howe are still remembered for their sewing machines, Blanchard's name is virtually unknown, perhaps because she was a woman in an age before feminism. Her inventions completely changed the industries dependent on hand-stitching by women. When she was economically secure, she spent time and money helping women who had been displaced by her machines.

Altogether, Blanchard received 28 patents over 45 years of inventing. Twenty-two of her patents involved sewing machines. She was often referred to as "Lady Edison," and is regarded as one of the greatest inventors of the industrial age, as well as one of the greatest women engineers of the era, despite having no formal engineering education.

GATUN LOCKS
PANAMA CANAL
1913

Interest in building a canal in Panama did not start with the French in the 19th century. The Spanish had considered building a canal to get the gold and other treasure they found in Peru, Ecuador, and Asia to Spanish ports more quickly. They surveyed the isthmus and drew up a plan for a canal in 1529, but wars in Europe kept them from carrying it out. The Spanish renewed their interest in 1819, and the Americans became interested when the Gold Rush started in 1848.

But nothing happened until 1876, when an international company was formed. That company failed within two years. Then the French stepped in, only to fail as well, causing a scandal in France that resulted in the conviction of several executives for fraud and mismanagement. By the end of French involvement, more than $260 million had been invested and more than 70 million cubic yards of earth had been excavated.

Enter the United States, which had been considering a canal through Nicaragua. A French engineer talked Congress out of Nicaragua and its volcanoes, and convinced them instead to buy the French interests in Panama, which they did for $40 million in 1902.

37

John Frank Stevens and the Panama Canal

THE PANAMA CANAL WAS A NIGHTMARE PROJECT THAT CLAIMED THE LIVES OF AT least 25,000 workers over the nearly two decades required to complete construction.

Two French companies tried and failed to create a canal between 1880 and 1893. Rampant diseases such as yellow fever and malaria, along with the difficulty of constructing a sea-level canal and insufficient experience on the part of the companies, ended their efforts. Around 22,000 deaths occurred between 1881 and 1889.

The first chief engineer chosen to construct the canal was John Findley Wallace, who lasted one year until he grew frustrated by the project. Next, President Theodore Roosevelt chose John Frank Stevens, an engineer with little formal education, but a career that included successful expansion of railroad lines, including the Great Northern Railway, across the U.S. Stevens was born on a farm near Gardiner, Maine, on April 25, 1853. He studied for just two years at the Farmington Normal School (now the University of Maine at Farmington).

Since job prospects were scarce, Stevens went west. Working in a city engineer's office in Minneapolis, he learned enough about civil engineering, surveying, and building railroads to describe himself as a practical engineer with a "bull-dog tenacity of purpose."

> In 1905, Stevens headed to Panama, took one look at the mess and decided that before excavating a canal, the area needed infrastructure, saying, "The digging is the least thing of all."

One of the first things he tackled was sanitation to control the mosquitoes that carried deadly diseases. Then he built warehouses, machine shops, and community housing for workers, as well as schools, hospitals, churches, and hotels. As a railroad man, he realized a railroad was essential for taking soil away from the excavations, so he rebuilt the Panama Railway, making it into an efficient system that could operate around the clock to remove the soil.

Besides creating a safe, livable environment for workers and solving the logistical problems of excavation, his most important contribution was to convince Roosevelt that a sea-level canal would not work and that it should instead be one of locks and dams.

Stevens said when he signed on that he would stay "until he could predict success or failure according to his own judgment." The reasons for his resignation twenty months after he began work were never made clear, but it was acknowledged by all that the project would never have been completed successfully if the engineers had stuck with the plan for a sea-level canal.

Not only was Stevens considered the foremost civil engineer of the time, but he also had approached the project as a humanitarian effort. Morale among the workers had been incredibly low until he arrived, but the efforts by Stevens to improve living conditions by introducing entertainment and better food paid off. He also eschewed his fancier living quarters to bunk with the workers. His constant cigar earned him the nickname "Big Smoke."

When he left, plans for the rest of the project were firmly in place. The workers were sorry to see their plain-spoken boss depart, and gave him a send-off "as if they were honoring a man who had already built the Panama Canal."

Lieutenant Colonel George Washington Goethals was the third and last chief engineer of the project from 1907 to its completion in 1914. He is referred to as "the Genius of the Panama Canal," but he always said he did not deserve the title, that his predecessor, Stevens, was the one who had actually earned it.

Stevens returned to his career in railroads in 1917, leading Woodrow Wilson's advisory committee of railway experts to Russia to help improve the Trans-Siberian and Chinese Eastern Railways until Allied troops were withdrawn. In 1919 he took leadership of the Inter-Allied Technical Board in Manchuria.

Even in retirement, he continued to receive honors for his various contributions to engineering. A few honors including the Distinguished Service Medal for service in Russia and the Franklin Medal. He built more than 1,000 miles of railroad during his time at Great Northern, and Stevens Pass in the Cascades is named for him. He died June 2, 1943, at age 90, in Southern Pines, North Carolina

Edna St. Vincent Millay and Louise Bogan

The work of these two women from Maine helped define poetry in the 20th century.

EDNA ST. VINCENT MILLAY WAS THE THIRD WOMAN TO WIN A PULITZER PRIZE, AND Louise Bogan was the fourth Poet Laureate of the United States. Born five years apart in the late 19th century, both moved away from Maine to advance their careers, although Millay's husband bought Ragged Island off the coast of Maine for her.

Edna St. Vincent Millay was born in Rockland, on February 22, 1892. Millay, known as "Vincent" to her family, was given her middle name for the New York hospital that had saved her uncle's life. Her mother and father divorced in 1899 and her mother raised the three daughters on her own, poverty forcing them to move from place to place, although she urged her offspring to participate in the arts as well as to be ambitious and self-sufficient.

They ended up in Camden, where Millay attended high school, had poetry published in the high school literary magazine and the local paper, the *Camden Herald*, and wrote the first poem that would bring her fame.

She submitted "Renascence" to a contest in *The Lyric Year* when she was twenty. When it took fourth place, everyone agreed her poem was best. The first-place winner called his win an "embarrassment," and the second-place winner offered to give her his prize money.

When wealthy arts patron Caroline B. Dow heard Millay recite her poetry and play piano at Camden's Whitehall Inn, she offered to pay tuition at Vassar College for Millay. Red-haired, beautiful, and openly bi-sexual, Millay was an early feminist. After graduation she moved to New York City and lived the Jazz-Age bohemian life in Greenwich Village. She wrote plays, including one opera libretto, as well as poetry, and worked

Edna St. Vincent Millay.

Louise Bogan.

with the Provincetown Players and the Theater Guild. She also wrote magazine pieces, satirical sketches, and short stories under the nom de plume, Nancy Boyd.

In 1923, Millay married Dutch businessman Eugene Jan Boissevain, the widower of labor lawyer and war correspondent Inez Mulholland, who was an early hero to Millay. Reports say the pair lived like "two bachelors," remaining "sexually open" for their 26-year marriage.

She was considered one of the most skillful writers of sonnets in the 20th century, combining traditional forms with modern attitudes. Her readings and performances were riveting and explored both progressive politics and sexuality, so her fame was greatly enhanced by her personality.

Her husband died of a stroke in 1949 at their New York farm, Steepletop. A year later, Millay died there of a heart attack. She was 58 years old. She remains one of America's most beloved poets. Steepletop is now a museum, as is the house in Rockland where she was born. The beginning of her poem "Renascence" appears on a plaque at the top of Camden's Mount Battie—fitting, since the poem describes the view from that very spot.

Millay caused a stir with her 1920 collection of poetry, *A Few Figs from Thistles,* because the work openly explored female sexuality and feminism. This work cemented her legend as a flippant rebel. It contains the poem "First Fig," with her famous line, "My candle burns at both ends." In 1923 she won the Pulitzer Prize for Poetry for *The Ballad of the Harp-Weaver.* Twenty years later, she won the Frost Medal for her lifetime contribution to American poetry, at the time only the sixth person and second woman to do so.

Louise Marie Bogan was born August 11, 1897, in Livermore Falls, to a mill-worker father. Her mother suffered from mental illness and flaunted her many affairs, a situation that tortured Louise for many years. Bogan fought depression for most of her life.

Like Millay, Bogan's intelligence prompted a benefactor to send her to school. In this case, Girls' Latin School in Boston. After that, she attended Boston University for a year, then gave up a scholarship to Radcliffe to marry an Army corporal, Curt Alexander. They had one daughter, Maidie Alexander, but the marriage ended in 1918 and Bogan moved to New York City. In 1920, Bogan went to Vienna for a few years to write.

When she returned to New York she published her first book of poetry in 1923, *Body of This Death*, followed by a second book, *Dark Summer*, in 1929. Soon after the second book, she was hired by *The New Yorker* as poetry editor and critic, a job she kept for 38 years. In the meantime, she married again in 1925 to poet and novelist Raymond Holden, a marriage that lasted twelve years.

Bogan and Millay were friends with many of the top poets and literary lions of their era, and most of their published works were written in the earlier parts of their lives. Bogan outlived Millay by many years and published a final collection of her poems, *Blue Estuaries*. An editor and critic as well as a poet, her prose has been described as direct, nonacademic, and sharp.

She died alone in New York City. Despite her long association with *The New Yorker,* her highly-praised poetry and criticism, and her deep, long-time friendships with other notable poets, Bogan always felt as though she was invisible in the literary world, even though some critics have called her the most accomplished woman poet of the 20th century. The advent of modern feminism has revived interest in her work.

Henry Knox

GENERAL HENRY KNOX, BORN IN 1850, STARTED LIFE IN POVERTY IN BOSTON. HIS father abandoned the family, six of his siblings died, and Henry had to drop out of Boston Latin School in fifth grade to help his mother make ends meet.

But Henry was smart and managed to educate himself by working in a book-bindery and saving up enough to open The London Book Shop in 1771. A voracious reader, he taught himself to speak and read French in order to read untranslated documents on his favorite topic: military tactics.

He joined a Boston militia before the Revolution and was spotted while on maneuvers on Boston Common by one of the most educated, aristocratic young women in the colonies, Lucy Flucker, of Boston and Philadelphia. She was smitten and quickly began to frequent his bookstore.

Her father, Thomas Flucker, was the Royal Secretary of the Province of Massachusetts and a loyalist to the Crown. Her parents disapproved of Lucy's match with the "genial giant" for many reasons, starting with politics and including the prospect of their daughter living in poverty, but the Fluckers finally relented and allowed the pair to marry in a quiet ceremony in June 1774.

In 1775, when the war broke out, Knox befriended General George Washington, abandoned his bookstore to looters, and joined the Continental Army, where he rose quickly to become chief artillery officer and accompanied Washington on most of his campaigns. Knox helped develop fortifications around Boston, directed the cannons

Knox witnessed the Boston Massacre in 1770 and tried to convince the British soldiers to return to their quarters. By 1772, he supported a group called the Sons of Liberty, which opposed British Colonial policies. He served on guard duty before the 1773 Boston Tea Party to be sure no tea was unloaded.

While Knox's military contributions were many, probably the one that turned the tide of the war was his brilliant fortification of Dorchester Heights in Boston. Knox is credited with suggesting the audacious plan to retrieve cannons captured from Fort Ticonderoga and Fort Crown Point in upstate New York and bring them to Boston.

Dubbed the "noble train of artillery," Knox and his men hauled sixty tons of cannon and other armaments 300 miles across deep snow and ice-covered rivers by ox-drawn sled. Several times the cannon broke through the river ice, but the men always managed to recover them. Planned for two weeks, the expedition took six weeks, reaching Cambridge on January 27, 1776.

Washington had recently taken the Dorchester Heights area, and the cannons were delivered to fortify the crucial hill, forcing the British to withdraw their fleet to Halifax.

at the Battle of Bunker Hill, and was one of two men chosen by General Washington to help lead the new army. Both he and Nathanael Greene stayed by Washington's side for the entire eight-and-a-half-year war.

Knox was also in charge of logistics during the famous crossing of the Delaware

River, during which he managed to get the men, horses, and artillery across the river without losing any. He crossed the river back again with all the same materiel and men, plus hundreds of prisoners. For this feat, he was elevated to brigadier general.

Near the war's end, Knox accompanied Washington's army south to direct placement and aiming of the artillery at the decisive Siege of Yorktown. He was promoted to be the Army's youngest major general in 1782.

In March of 1785, Knox was tapped to be the first Secretary of War of the new republic, where he helped to form the United States Army and establish a military academy. He is credited with being the first to use the term "Father of Your Country" in reference to Washington, and with giving Washington the outline for the new government that was eventually adopted.

MONTPELIER

Henry Knox retired to Maine in 1795 and built his mansion, Montpelier, in Thomaston, on land Lucy had inherited from her family, 576,000 acres known as the Waldo Patent. He involved himself in several business ventures, including shipping timber, quarrying lime, making bricks, building canals on the local Georges River, and experimenting with agriculture.

Henry's ventures took a long time to succeed and in the meantime, the family fortunes dwindled. Henry choked on a chicken bone, developed an infection, and died three days later, on October 25, 1806 at age 56.

Lucy died in 1824, and Montpelier remained in the family until it was razed in 1871 to make room for a railroad. One original brick building remains and now houses the Thomaston Historical Society. An exact replica of the three-story, nineteen-room Montpelier was built in 1929 and serves as a museum containing many of the estate's original treasures.

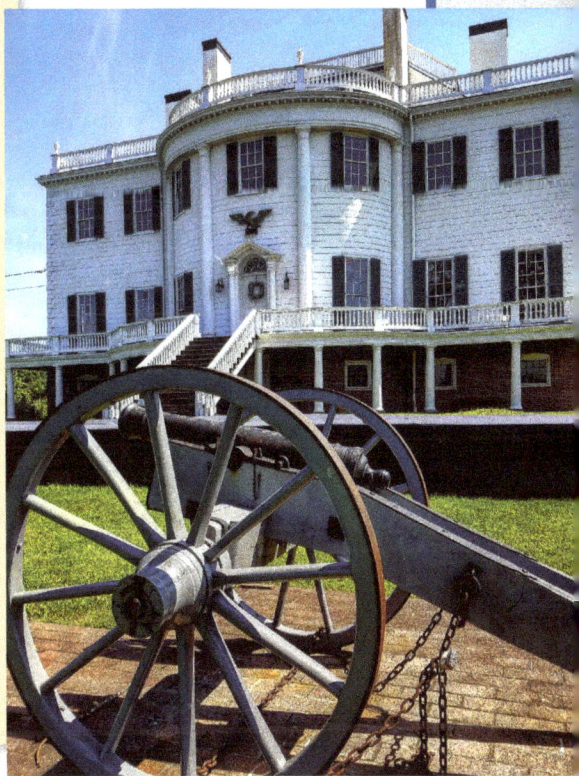

40

Artemus Ward

ARTEMUS WARD LIVED FAST AND HARD DURING HIS CAREER BOTH HERE AND ABROAD. It's a good thing his candle burned brightly because it burned out completely when he was only 32 years old.

Born Charles Farrar Brown in Waterford in 1834, he was apprenticed to a printer at age thirteen, and set type for several New England newspapers before getting a job with a Boston paper in 1851.

He began writing humorous sketches at an early age for dailies and weeklies, starting with the "Boston Carpet-bag," and signing them, "Chub." His style included purposeful misspellings, malapropisms, grammatical errors, and bizarre sentence constructions.

When he moved to Cleveland, Ohio, he began the first of his Artemus Ward series for the *Plain Dealer*. Later, the series was collected into a book that won him great popularity in the U.S. and England. When he achieved notoriety, he added an "e" to his last name, making it Browne.

"Browne saw neither the table, nor the chair, nor any person who might be near, nothing, in fact, but the funny pictures which were tumbling out of his brain. When writing, his gaunt form looked ridiculous enough. One leg hung over the arm of his chair like a great hook, while he would write away, sometimes laughing to himself, and then slapping the table in the excess of his mirth."
—Plain Dealer *colleague George Hoyt describing Browne's writing technique*

In 1860, Browne was hired as editor of *Vanity Fair*, then a humor weekly in New York. The magazine failed by 1862, the year his first book was published, and Browne started giving humorous lectures as Artemus Ward, attracting large audiences as he portrayed an illiterate rube possessed of Yankee common sense.

Brett Harte was in the audience the first night Ward performed in San Francisco, and later described the event as "humor that belongs to the country of boundless prairies, limitless rivers, and stupendous cataracts—that fun which overlies the surface of our national life . . ."

Later, when Ward played Virginia City, Nevada, he met Mark Twain and they formed an immediate friendship that included participating in drunken antics and nearly getting arrested. Ward was instrumental in getting Twain's first piece published, "The Celebrated Jumping Frog of Calaveras County." Twain credited Ward with this and with his influence on Twain's future style, arguably the start of standup comedy in the U.S.

Described by friends as good-natured, incapable of malice, quick to make friends, and a "pure Bohemian," the written words of Browne/Ward were enhanced greatly by his performance on stage when infused with his personality. He was reportedly Abraham Lincoln's favorite author. Just prior to presenting the Emancipation Proclamation to his cabinet in 1862, Lincoln read them Ward's newest episode, "Outrage in Utiky."

> In Ward's day, lectures were a popular form of entertainment, although they were serious affairs on topics such as literature, science, philosophy and travel. Ward turned the genre on its head, by appearing across the country as a serious lecturer wearing a dour expression, but spouting outrageous nonsense, such as referring to his extremely gifted, but non-existent piano player who "always wore mittens when playing the piano."

**Let us all be happy and live within our means,
even if we have to borrow the money to do it with.**

In 1866, Ward/Browne traveled to London where he performed his latest show, "The Babes in the Wood." In London he made friends with the crowd from the humor magazine, *Punch*. True to form, he partied nightly after performances, and in only two months his health deteriorated to the point where he often couldn't finish his performances. In March of 1867, he died of tuberculosis. He is buried in Elm Vale Cemetery in Waterford.

41

Taber Drop-Axle Wagon

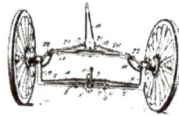

719,581. WAGON-GEAR. Silas W. Taber, Houlton, Me. Filed Jan. 17, 1902. Serial No. 90,192. (No model.)

SILAS W. TABER OF HOULTON LIVED IN MAINE'S LARGEST COUNTY, AROOSTOOK, WHICH is still the agricultural center of Maine and source of the state's biggest crop, the potato.

Before Taber came up with the U-shaped drop-axle, the straight axle of farm wagons meant the larger the wheels, the higher the wagon bed had to ride above them. The high wagons, loaded with potato barrels, were unsteady in the rutted fields and difficult for horses to pull.

Employing ball bearings, a truss-bar that kept the axle straight, and U-shaped front and rear axles that allowed the wheel bed to ride below the height of the wheel hubs, Taber revolutionized the wagons farmers used all the time. The drop axle made the center of gravity lower, making it easier for horses to pull and making the wagon more stable.

Potato farmers loaded barrels with potatoes in the field onto the wagons which the horses then pulled back to the potato houses for transport or storage. The lower profile made the farmers' work of loading potatoes in the field easier as well. Wagons could have employed smaller wheels in order to ride lower to the ground, but the high wheels were better for the rutted roads and farm field conditions.

Taber was granted a patent in 1902 for his truss-supported axle and a "king pin" brace that improved the drop-axle he was already producing in his factory on Mechanic Street. His business card had begun advertising the drop-axle wagon in 1900.

Raised in Old Town, Taber was taught blacksmithing by his father, who moved the family to Houlton in 1865. Silas built his own shop in 1871, making and repairing horseshoes, tools, and other metal implements. He also built custom wagons for farmers, as did his father.

What a Taber Wagon Will Do !

75 Barrels Potatoes hauled by one pair of Horses 3 miles to market on a road with a number of heavy grades. Sept. 15, 1909

ze : } 2 In front axle } Roller Bearing
     } 2 1-4 hind axle }

McCluskey Bros. Hardware Co.

Sole Agents, Houlton, Maine

For Sale by

His three-story Taber Wagon factory boasted a blacksmith shop on the ground floor, a woodworking shop where the wagon bodies were constructed on the second floor, and a paint shop on the third floor. Outside the factory building, he had a wheel jig where wagon wheels were assembled and the steel tires were mounted.

Unfortunately for Taber, his invention was overtaken by the gasoline-powered tractor and when he died in 1912, manufacture of his wagons ended.

42

Breech-Loading Rifle

JOHN HANCOCK HALL, A PORTLAND NATIVE, IS BEST REMEMBERED FOR HIS invention of a breech-loading rifle that could be mass produced with interchangeable parts. A professor of technology thinks Hall might be Maine's most important inventor because of his overall contributions to mass-production, which influenced all segments of American industry.

Hall was born in Portland on January 4, 1781, where his father, a Harvard graduate, likely tutored him until he was thirteen, when his father died. This may have been Hall's only formal education.

As a youngster, Hall worked in his father's tannery. He may also have had some involvement in boat- building, but the only known account is a partnership in a privateer launched in 1812 that was lost. At age twenty-two, he joined the newly formed Portland Light Infantry, an independent militia. This is where his interest in firearms was piqued.

His mother died and Hall assumed responsibility for raising his two younger brothers and a sister. A year later he applied for a $750 loan, listing his occupation as cooper. Meanwhile, all along he had been experimenting with guns in his spare time, especially working on the speed of loading them. In 1811, he invented a single-shot, breech-loading flintlock rifle, which he patented along with architect William Thornton.

Upon completion of his first government contract in 1825, Hall invited the U.S. Ordnance Department to check out his system. Besides the rifles themselves, officials were impressed with his other inventions, saying they could provide "the most beneficial results to the country, especially if carried into effect on a large scale." Firing tests also proved Hall's rifles to be more accurate than the other weapons available to the army at the time..

Hall informed President James Madison of it in a letter, saying the firearm would, " . . . enable a man to load a rifle either lying on the ground or sitting on horseback in less time and with less trouble than is now taken in loading smooth bore guns standing on foot."

Hall manufactured around fifty of his rifles a year. The U.S. Army Ordnance Corps expressed interest and ordered 200 rifles, but Hall had to refuse the contract because he knew he could not deliver by the 1815 deadline.

So he turned his attention to figuring out how to manufacture his rifles faster, recognizing that interchangeably fitted parts, or what he called the "uniformity principle," were the key to increased production. Prior to this, guns were manufactured by hand, one piece at a time. In 1816, he informed the Army of his new concept and the War Department ordered 1,000 of his "Model of 1819" rifles, conditioned on the concept of interchangeable parts working.

The contract impelled Hall to move to Harpers Ferry Arsenal in West Virginia, where he spent five years in an old sawmill manufacturing the rifles. The water-power of the sawmill enabled him to experiment with new machine tools in order to make the parts truly interchangeable.

Using the water power to run belts and pulleys that operated metal cutters and saws, Hall managed to make consistent parts that could be hand-filed by barely skilled workers. He also invented a gauge system to measure the consistency of the parts.

Workers trained in Hall's techniques on the sophisticated machines and systems transferred these methods and skills to the manufacturing of all kinds of other items, including shoes, bicycles, typewriters, railway equipment, clocks, clothing, watches, and later, to automobiles. His straight-cutting machine was the forerunner of the widely-used milling machine

Hall retired from Harper's Ferry in 1840 after twenty successful years and died in Randolph County, Missouri, on February 26, 1841.

Merritt Roe Smith, a history of technology professor at the Massachusetts Institute of Technology, wrote a book about Hall, in which he said Hall may be Maine's most important inventor for his contributions not only to the gun industry, but to the entire manufacturing industry.

"He had a set of very sophisticated gauges and very innovative machinery. Mass production would not be possible without Hall and those components," Smith said.

43

Madame Nordica

BORN LILLIAN "LILLIE" NORTON IN A FARMHOUSE IN FARMINGTON ON DECEMBER 12, 1857, her future was predicted at age seven by a neighbor commonly thought to be a witch.

> According to lore, "Aunt Eunice" took little Lillie's hand in hers and told her she would "sail the seven seas, and the crowned heads of Europe will bow before you." She was right.

In 1889, La Nordica met the widow of Richard Wagner, Cosima, who was looking for a soprano to fill the role of Elsa in Wagner's *Lohengrin*. Critics doubted an American could adequately perform the German role, but in 1894, La Nordica wowed them as the first American to sing at Bayreuth. For the next two decades, she became renowned for her Wagnerian heroines.

Unable to make a living on the farm, the Norton family moved to Boston, where her father established a photography studio and her mother went to work in a department store. At fourteen, Lillie began her musical studies and went on to the New England Conservatory.

Immediately upon graduation, Lillie was invited to tour Europe with bandleader Patrick Gilmore. Her mother accompanied her on the four-year trip that included appearances in London and Paris. When the tour reached Milan, Italy, an Italian voice coach reinterpreted her name as "Lily of the North" and translated it into Italian as *Giglio Nordica*, which soon became *La Nordica*.

It was the Golden Age of opera, and she quickly became a favorite in Italy and was invited to Russia, where she performed for the likes of Count Leo Tolstoy and Czar Alexander II. Accolades at the Paris Opera followed performances there. By then she had fame and admirers and returned home to tour the United States with a British company, "Her Majesty's Opera Company," finally returning to London.

The beautiful La Nordica performed many concerts outside the opera. Besides coming to hear her great voice, audiences also attended her concerts to see her stunning Paris gowns and magnificent jewels, often given to her by admirers.

La Nordica was planning to retire to Farmington, but she went on a South Pacific tour first. After a successful performance in Melbourne, Australia, she sailed on the *Tasman*, which was wrecked on a coral reef. After three days, the ship was rescued by a Japanese coal boat, but La Nordica suffered from hypothermia. She was eventually brought to what is now Jakarta, Indonesia, where she remained ill for months until she was carried off by pneumonia. She died on May 10, 1914.

Few of her commercial recordings exist, and even fewer are good. This may be because of the primitive recording equipment. However, two recorded excerpts—from *La Gioconda* and *Il Trovatore* remain, and are considered quite remarkable. A few recordings on wax cylinders from live performances at the Metropolitan Opera between 1901 and 1903 are the best surviving recordings. Marston Records released a CD of her recordings in 2003.

The house where she was born is now the Nordica Homestead Museum, listed on the National Register of Historic Places. Her sisters, Annie and Onie, gave the

The first advertising for Coca-Cola appears in national magazines.

Annual sales of Coca-Cola hit the 1 million-gallon mark.

Lillian Nordica, noted opera singer, begins to endorse Coca-Cola and appears in nationwide advertising in 1905.

1904 1905 1906

Coca-Cola

Love the new

house to Lillian for her birthday in 1911 and furnished it with as many items as they could from their time living there. It also contains many items of memorabilia of her career—including gowns and stage jewelry—as well as a library of books in which she appears.

Local legend says her ghost haunts the Nordica Auditorium, named for her at the University of Farmington. August 17 is Nordica Day, and every year on this day the Nordica Scholarship is awarded at her namesake auditorium to a singer studying in Maine for a classical career.

Lillian was one of the first celebrity endorsers, her image appeared on trays, calendars, placemats, and belt buckles for the Coca Cola Company in 1905. She endorsed her record label, the Columbia Phonograph Co., then lent her name to "weight-reducing" bath salts, called Madame Nordica's Bath Powder, and also endorsed Steinway pianos and Fowler bicycles.

44

M.A.S.H.

THE KOREAN WAR TOOK THREE YEARS, BUT IT TOOK DR. H. RICHARD HORNBERGER of Bremen, Maine, twelve years to write his humorous, semi-autobiographical novel, *MASH*, about serving as a doctor in a Mobile Army Surgical Hospital during the war.

> The book spawned a wildly successful movie and an even more successful TV show that ran for eleven years on CBS. It was one of the most popular shows in television history.

When Hornberger finished his book, the manuscript was rejected by several publishers, so he worked with sportswriter W.C. Heinz to rewrite it. William Morrow and Company bought it and published it in 1968 under the *nom de plume* Richard Hooker.

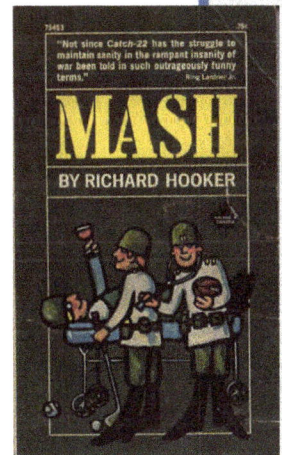

It was a great success, so successful that the movie came out in 1970, was nominated for five Academy Awards, and won for Best Adapted Screenplay. It won the Grand Prix award at the 1970 Cannes Film Festival, was chosen for preservation in the U.S. National Film Registry, and was designated "culturally significant" by the Library of Congress. It also won Best Motion Picture at the Golden Globes in 1971.

While the book and movie were huge hits with the American public as well as international audiences, they were not such a big hit with the book's author. H. Richard Hornberger was born in Trenton, New Jersey, on February 1, 1924, and attended Bowdoin College in Maine. After graduation, he studied medicine at Cornell Medical School and joined the U.S. Army as a surgeon in the Army Medical Corps during the Korean War.

Captain Hornberger served in the 8055th MASH in Korea, which was turned into the fictional 4077th MASH unit for the book. After the war he worked briefly for

Although the movie and TV series clearly identified the setting as the Korean War, the series ran during the Vietnam War and had an unmistakable undertone referencing Vietnam. Hornberger reportedly liked the movie because he thought it followed his original intent, the 'regular Army' vs. enlistees. But he was a conservative Republican and thoroughly disliked the liberal, antiwar political attitude of the TV series, particularly the characterization of the main character, Hawkeye, as portrayed by Alan Alda. He refused to watch it, and has been quoted as saying, "I don't hold with this anti-war nonsense." Hornberger repeatedly said that he did not write an antiwar book, but a fictionalized memoir of his work in Korea that balanced black humor with the seriousness and difficulty of the work.

The original cast of the *M.A.S.H.* television series.

a Veterans Administration hospital, then moved to Broad Cove in Bremen, Maine, and practiced thoracic surgery until he retired. A fellow doctor described Hornberger as "a very good surgeon with a tremendous sense of humor."

Hornberger co-wrote two other books, *MASH Goes to Maine* and *MASH Mania*, and lent his name to a series of MASH books written by William E. Butterworth. None of them achieved the commercial success of the original.

Hornberger died in a Portland hospital of leukemia at age 73, on November 4, 1997. After his death, Hornberger's home was offered for sale at public auction. His alma mater, Bowdoin College, holds a typescript manuscript of *MASH*, annotated with editor's corrections, in its library's Special Collections and Archives.

45

Margaret Knight

THE 19TH CENTURY WAS A GREAT TIME FOR INVENTORS WITHOUT MUCH FORMAL education. Margaret Knight was one of these, and, in fact, has been called "the most famous 19th-century woman inventor;" and her newspaper obituary dubbed her a "female Edison."

She was born in York on February 14, 1838, to James Knight and Hannah Teal. Her dad died when she was small, so she dropped out of school at age twelve to work in a cotton mill for six years. Her two older brothers were already working in mills.

During her early childhood in Maine she designed and built mechanical toys for her brothers using her father's old tools. She made a foot warmer for her mother who often stayed up late sewing, and made kites and sleds for her brothers. Neighborhood kids paid her to make them special things.

When she was eleven, Knight visited a mill in Manchester, New Hampshire, and witnessed a terrible accident involving a shuttle flying off a loom and severely injuring a worker. She went home to the book of ideas she kept, and invented a stop-motion device that would immediately stop the machine if something caught in it. This device was put to use in the factory immediately and is credited with saving many lives, but at the time, neither Knight nor her family knew enough to apply for a patent.

Queen Victoria decorated Knight for her invention of the paper bag machine, which quickly became popular all over Europe as well as in the United States. Now they are in use all over the world.

Knight later founded a paper-bag making company—the Eastern Paper Bag Co.—with a Massachusetts businessman and finally started earning enough money

Knight's first patent is also the invention she is most noted for. She had moved to Springfield, Massachusetts, to work in a paper bag factory and saw the need for a flat-bottomed bag that would stand up while being filled. She designed one, then designed a device to fold and glue the paper. She built a wooden model of her invention, but in order to apply for a patent, she needed an iron model.

While her model was being built at a Boston machine shop, a worker there stole her design and applied for a patent himself. When Knight applied for her patent, she was told Charles Annan was ahead of her. But Knight fought back, filing a patent interference lawsuit. Fortunately, she had all the drawings for every step of the machine's development, bits from the failed versions, and witnesses. Annan's entire argument in court was that a woman couldn't possibly have invented such a complicated device. Some reports say the court actually laughed out loud before awarding the patent to Knight. Her machine is still in use today and the original she built is in the Smithsonian.

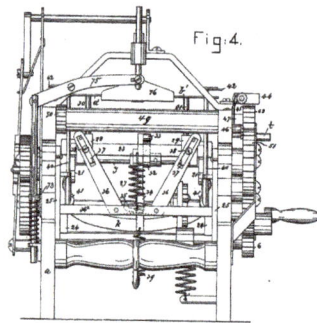
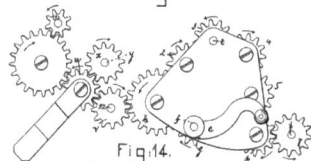

Knight's first patent was for a machine to make flat-bottomed paper bags.

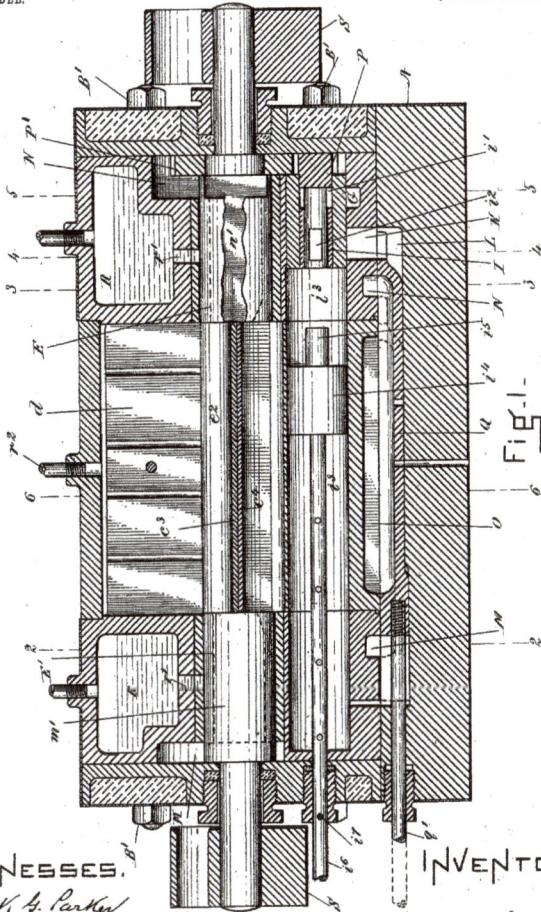

No. 720,818.

PATENTED FEB. 17, 1903.

M. E. KNIGHT.
ROTARY ENGINE.
APPLICATION FILED JUNE 16, 1902.

NO MODEL.

5 SHEETS—SHEET 1.

Fig. 1.

WITNESSES.
Frank G. Parker
A. L. Robinson

INVENTOR.
Margaret E. Knight

Margaret Knight's patent diagram of a rotary engine.

to be comfortable, if not wealthy. Sexism still plagued Knight in her own company. Men on the factory floor would not follow her directions until she demonstrated her skill on the machine.

Knight never married and died on October 12, 1914, in Framingham, Massachusetts, at the age of 76, leaving an estate of $275.05. She was one of the most productive female inventors and was inducted into the National Inventors Hall of Fame, the first woman to receive this honor, in 2006.

Being a strict disciplinarian, Edward Preble established a code of 106 rules covering shipboard conduct. Many of the best young officers of the era served under Preble and were shaped by his rules of order. Preble's rules imposed a discipline the old Continental Navy had sadly lacked. When he was first assigned these young officers, Preble called them, "nothing but a pack of boys." Later, they proudly called themselves "Preble's Boys." Most were highly successful in later wars, especially the War of 1812, and still rank among the Navy's most famous officers. Preble's rules formed the basis of the Naval officer corps as it still exists today. Besides expecting strict discipline among his crew, he also insisted his ships be ready for any type of action at all times while under sail. This was something other naval officers of the time did not require. In 2002, the sixth U.S. naval vessel named for him, the guided missile destroyer USS *Preble*, was commissioned.

46

Edward Preble

THE ONLY REASON EDWARD PREBLE WASN'T BORN IN MAINE IS BECAUSE PORTLAND was Falmouth, Massachusetts, on August 15, 1761. The boy who was to become one of the leading lights of the U.S. Navy saw his home destroyed when the British burned Falmouth to the ground. Many believe this event led him to run away to sea at age sixteen. He joined the crew of a privateer, and by 1779 was made a midshipman in the Massachusetts State Navy, stationed aboard the 26-gun ship *Protector*. When the vessel was captured by the British, Preble spent time aboard a prison ship. Soon after he was released, Preble was assigned to the sloop *Winthrop*.

> During a battle off Castine the following year, Preble showed the mettle for which he would become famous throughout the Navy. He swept in, boarded a moored enemy brig with a small number of men, took the crew hostage, and captured the ship while the British fired on them from the shore.

After the Revolutionary War, the Continental Navy was disbanded and Preble went into the merchant marine for fifteen years. But in April 1798, with war threatening, he was commissioned a lieutenant in the U.S. Navy. A year later he was given command of the USS *Pickering*, a 14-gun brig. Preble took his ship to the West Indies during the quasi-war with France in order to protect U.S. commerce. Promoted to captain in June 1799, he was given command of the frigate USS *Essex*.

Around this time, the United States was having a bit of a spat with Tripoli. Barbary Coast pirates had for three centuries been preying on merchant ships from all over the world. Most countries either paid the ransom or simply paid an annual fee to the sultans for free passage of their vessels in the Mediterranean. Since England paid the yearly tribute, the American colonial ships were covered, but when independence came, U.S. vessels were unprotected.

At first, the U.S. made treaties with the sultans and paid the modest tribute, but in 1801 the pasha of of Tripoli, Yusuf Karamanli, decided to demand a higher tribute

THE START OF THE BARBARY WAR

In October 1803, Captain William Bainbridge ran his frigate, the *Philadelphia*, aground near Tripoli Harbor while trying to intercept two pirate ships. Although he dumped the cannons and cut down a mast, he couldn't right the vessel. So he surrendered the ship and crew to the pirates. Commodore Preble decided the only recourse was to destroy the *Philadelphia* to prevent the pirates from using her. He sent 25-year-old Lieutenant Stephen Decatur to lead the night mission with seventy volunteers, sailing a captured corsair, and employing a pilot who spoke Arabic.

Pretending to be a disabled pirate ship, they asked permission to tie up to the *Philadelphia*. Their ruse was quickly discovered, but the Americans had already boarded the *Philadelphia*. They engaged in hand-to-hand combat with the pirates, retook the ship, set fire to her, and escaped. Decatur was elevated to full captain, the youngest captain in the U.S. Navy.

of President Thomas Jefferson. Jefferson never liked the idea of paying the pirates, so he sent a fleet of three frigates and a sloop to Gibraltar under the command of Commodore Richard Dale. When Dale arrived, he learned Tripoli had already declared war on the United States.

Rather than engage in battle around the well-protected harbor, Dale had the fleet form a blockade of Tripoli and act as escort to merchant vessels. A year later, Dale resigned and was replaced by Commodore Richard Morris. Even though his orders were to engage the enemy, he chose to continue a passive blockade. He was recalled in 1803 and fired by an angry Jefferson.

In June of that year, now Commodore Preble was given command of the fleet and its flagship, the USS *Constitution*. By October, the First Barbary War had become a reality.

Preble realized he would need shallow-draft vessels to attack Tripoli Harbor, so he borrowed six small gunboats and two bomb ketches from the king of the Two Sicilies. He then attacked Tripoli. Although the borrowed boats were outnumbered, the Americans captured three pirate gunboats, sunk three more, bombarded the shore from the *Constitution,* and turned their guns on the pasha's castle.

Following each of four more attacks in the month of August, Preble offered to negotiate and ransom the captured crew of the *Philadelphia*. Karamanli refused and the attacks continued. A plan to explode a vessel in the middle of the Tripoli harbor and have the American crew escape, went awry. The pirates fired on the vessel, blowing it up with the crew aboard. When Commodore Samuel Barron arrived with reinforcements, he outranked Preble and took command of the fleet. Preble was insulted by what he considered a demotion, and returned to the U.S. a hero.

Upon his return in 1805, Preble was awarded a gold medal for "gallantry and good conduct" for the actions of his squadron in Tripoli. In 1806, Jefferson offered him the job of Secretary of the Navy. Problem declined, citing poor health, and instead became involved in shipbuilding duties in Portland and as a naval advisor to Jefferson. On August 25, 1807, Preble died of a gastrointestinal illness at age 46, and was buried in Portland's Eastern Cemetery.

47

Dorothea Dix

DOROTHEA DIX, WAS BORN IN HAMDEN, MAINE, BUT TRAVELED THE WORLD AS A teacher and activist. She was a leading figure in national and international movements to bring reform to the indigent mentally ill.

By 1880, Dorothea Dix had a legacy of 123 hospitals throughout the U.S., plus fifteen schools for the "feeble-minded," a school for the blind, and many training schools for nurses. Her work on improved conditions served to prove that all mental illness was not incurable and also inspired the creation of many more such facilities.

Born April 4, 1802 to alcoholic parents, her father, an itinerant Methodist preacher, was also abusive—although he did teach her to read. Just before Hamden fell to the British in the War of 1812, the family escaped to Worcester, Massachusetts, where Dorothea's two brothers were born and their care fell to Dorothea.

When Dix was twelve, she and her brothers went to live with her wealthy paternal grandmother in Boston, where she read her grandfather's Harvard textbooks. In 1821, at age sixteen, Dix opened a school for the children of wealthy families—she taught poor children at her home.

She opened another Boston school for girls in 1831 and ran it for five years until she fell ill. A doctor recommended a trip to Europe for her health, and while there she met some of the pioneers of improvements in mental health treatment.

An inheritance left to Dix when her grandmother died in 1837 allowed her to continue her work. She returned to Massachusetts, studied care for the insane poor throughout the state, and noted the widespread abuse of mentally ill patients within the underfunded and unregulated jail system. The conditions she witnessed caused her to abandon her teaching career to work as a nurse and advocate.

"I proceed, Gentlemen, briefly to call your attention to the present state of Insane Persons confined within this Commonwealth, in cages, stalls, pens! Chained, naked, beaten with rods, and lashed into obedience."
—*from Dorothea Dix's report to the Massachusetts Legislature*

At the time women could not vote, hold office, or testify before a legislature, so Dix had to ask a male representative to read her report. After helping pass a reform bill in Massachusetts in 1843, Dix moved on to New Jersey, where she conducted a similar inventory of conditions at jails. Again she helped to effect reform in 1845, when the legislature passed a bill to establish a state asylum.

Her success led her to conduct similar investigations in other states from New Hampshire to Louisiana. She prevailed in establishing asylums in Illinois, North Carolina, and Pennsylvania.

Dix was finally able to convince the federal government, too, and Congress passed a bill setting aside 12,225,000 acres to establish facilities for the "blind, deaf, and dumb." The Bill for the Benefit of the Indigent Insane passed both houses but was vetoed by President Franklin Pierce, who wanted the states to take sole responsibility for the care of their residents.

Dix returned to Europe in 1855 and traveled through thirteen countries, working with other activists to achieve changes in the treatment of the mentally ill as she had in the U.S. Back home, she traveled to the states she had missed the first time around and finally managed to establish at least 32 hospitals in New Jersey, Indiana, Kentucky, Missouri, Tennessee, Mississippi, Louisiana, North Carolina, and Maryland.

When the Civil War broke out in 1861, Dix was 59. Still, she offered her services to the

Dorothea's bossy style as the Army's superintendent of nurses earned her the nickname, "Dragon Dix." She was widely disliked by the nurses who worked under her. She reportedly required that her nurses be over age thirty, plain, and wear dull uniforms. One of her nurses was Louisa May Alcott, later the author of *Little Women*. Alcott said Dix was respected but not well-liked and that nurses would "steer clear" of her.

The Dorothea Dix Museum on the grounds of the Harrisburg State Hospital in Pennsylvania.

War Department. Though she had never trained as a nurse, she convinced military officials a women could handle the job, and she was appointed superintendent of Union Army Nurses.

Dix attracted up to 3,000 women to the Army, made sure they were treated properly, and there was no question that efficiency and quality of

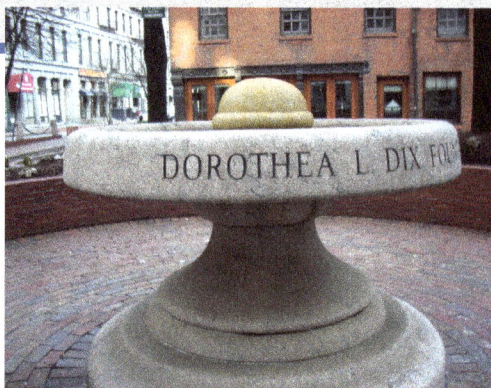

The fountain for thirsty horses Dix gave to the city of Boston to honor the Massachusetts Society for the Prevention of Cruelty to Animals.

care improved under her supervision. She also made sure her nurses cared for both Union and Confederate soldiers equally, earning her respect in the South. Her nurses were often the only caretakers available to Confederate soldiers.

Dix's personal biases affected her ability to do her work during the war. Thousands of Catholic nuns served successfully as army nurses, but Dix didn't trust Catholics so had difficulty working with Irish and German nurses. Losing influence to the likes of Clara Barton and Dr. Mary Edwards Walker, she quit in 1865, considering her war experience a failure.

Despite her advocacy for women's education, Dorothea Dix never lent her support and considerable fame to the feminist movement. She was also criticized for her failure to support abolition. Although she had little to do with the organization, Dix was elected "President for Life" of the Army Nurses Association, a social club for Civil War volunteer nurses. She was honored by the U.S. Post Office with a stamp in 1983. In Maine, the Bangor Mental Health Institute was renamed for her in 2006. She is noted on the Boston Women's Heritage Trail, and, on Venus there's a crater named Dix in her honor.

> "If I am cold, they are cold; if I am weary, they are distressed; if I am alone, they are abandoned."
> —*Dix writing on her work for the mentally ill*

After the war, she returned to her work to improve the lot of prisoners, the disabled, and the mentally ill, especially in the south. In 1881, she retired to a private suite in the New Jersey State Hospital, where she continued her correspondence with reformers around the world. Dix died in New Jersey on July 17, 1887 at the age of 85 and was buried in Mount Auburn Cemetery in Cambridge, Massachusetts.

Fly Rod Crosby

IN A DAY WHEN WOMEN RARELY ACHIEVED FAME, ESPECIALLY FOR PURSUITS CON-sidered to be strictly the province of men, Cornelia Thurza "Fly Rod" Crosby was a true anachronism. The one who became famous for her outdoor activities, such as fly fishing, had an unlikely start as a sportswoman.

She was born November 10, 1854, in Phillips, just south of the Rangeley Lakes region. Tuberculosis struck her family, killing her father when Cornelia was little. The disease also affected Cornelia, leaving her sickly throughout her life. Her older brother died from it in 1868 at the age of 23.

In her teens, she inherited $600 and used it to attend a girls' school in Augusta. She then went to work as a bank teller, but the recurring sick spells that left her bedridden forced her to take a lot of time off to recuperate. A doctor once told her she would die without "abundant doses of fresh air."

When she was 24 years old, she was taken to the foot of Mount Blue, where she went fishing and caught her first "speckled beauty," as she called Maine's trout. And thus from a sickly young woman, a fly-fishing legend was born.

Farmington fishing rod maker Charles E. Wheeler gave Crosby a

Maine Central Railroad saw an opportunity in Fly Rod Crosby's popularity and hired her to promote the outdoor industry, rather than the railroad itself. Fly Rod had dubbed Maine, "The Nation's Playground," and the railroad figured it was a better way to attract tourists who would then use the railroad to get to the places Fly Rod wrote about. She attracted thousands to the Maine woods with her writing. Her biographers subtitled their book about her, "The Woman Who Marketed Maine."

bamboo rod and she quickly became an expert, catching 200 fish in one day. According to some reports, she caught 2,500 trout during the summer of 1893. She became a regular fixture in Rangeley during fishing season and her reputation as an angler spread. By 1886, she had earned the nickname "Fly Rod" locally.

She began to write a weekly column, "Fly Rod's Notebook" for the local *Phillips Phonograph* on outdoor sports, mostly about her own fishing adventures. Her column was syndicated in newspapers around the country, including in New York, Boston, and Chicago. Her fame and popularity grew, as did interest in hunting and fishing opportunities in Maine. Her chatty column included information about where to stay and descriptions of sporting camps.

In 1895, Crosby organized Maine's exhibit at the first Sportsmen's Exposition in New York's Madison Square Garden. The following year, she shocked the attendees when she appeared in a green leather hunting outfit that sported a mid-calf length skirt—at the time fairly scandalous. She completed the outfit with a tailored jacket, a red sweater, a peaked red and green hat, and a pair of green lace-up boots. Crowds thronged to watch her fly-fishing demonstrations and stayed to hear her describe the wonders of Maine's great outdoors.

Her displays at the expositions included a log cabin, taxidermy, and fish tanks with live salmon and trout. She met Annie Oakley at the 1896 show and they became fast friends. For roughly a decade, she attended the New York shows and other similar shows in Boston and Philadelphia.

She had been hired by the Maine Fish and Game Association to lobby the Maine Legislature to register the state's hunting and fishing guides. While she was attending the Sportsmen's Exposition in 1897, she received word that a bill had passed requiring a license for guides and some funds to protect fish and game in Maine.

In 1898, Crosby was awarded license number 1, making her the first official Registered Maine Guide.

Changing technology took a toll on her career when automobiles and trucks began to replace railroads as the primary method of transport. In 1936, Maine Central shut down, tore up the tracks, and sold whatever they could. In her older years, she wrote a lot about conserving natural resources for later generations by placing bag limits on deer, salmon, and trout. She also advocated for a catch and release fishing program.

She suffered a knee injury in 1899 which caused her great emotional distress and physical pain. Her fishing and hunting were greatly reduced and her writing decreased during her time in and out of hospitals. Despite her sickliness and the near-blindness that affected her, Crosby lived to be 92, dying on November 11, 1946. The *Rangeley Record* ended her obituary this way: "Rangeley has lost one of its most famous people and America has lost its most famous woman sportsman. May her soul rest in peace."

The Fly Rod Crosby Trail, honoring the Maine hero, starts in Phillips and continues 45 miles through the communities of the region. Built and maintained by volunteers, the trail aims to show the area as seen through Crosby's writings. There are sections for hiking, biking, ATV riding, and kayaking, with signs to explain the natural and cultural history. The Phillips Historical Society houses a lot of Crosby's writings and paraphernalia, including photographs, the tea set that accompanied her on fishing trips, and the sign that hung outside her house in Phillips that read, "St. Anthony's Cottage."

Fly Rod Crosby served as a model of independence and athleticism for young women everywhere. She was renowned, honored, and enjoyed the status of a legend for many years of her life, but she was modest, once describing herself as "a plain woman of uncertain age, standing six feet in my stockings . . . I scribble a bit for various sporting journals, and I would rather fish any day than go to heaven."

Samantha Smith

BROWN-HAIRED, BLUE-EYED, AND POSSESSED OF A BIG, OPEN SMILE, TEN-YEAR-old Samantha Smith of Manchester, grew concerned about United States-Russian relations and the fate of the planet soon after Yuri Andropov was chosen the new Soviet premier in 1982.

"Actually, the whole thing started when I asked my mother if there was going to be a war," said Samantha Smith in an interview. "There was always something on television about missiles and nuclear bombs. Once I watched a science show on public television and the scientists said that a nuclear war would wreck the Earth and destroy the atmosphere. Nobody would win a nuclear war. I woke up one morning and wondered if this was going to be the last day of the Earth."

"If everyone is so afraid of him, why don't they ask him if he is going to start a war," Smith asked her mother, Jane, suggesting her mom write to Andropov to ask him directly; but her mother suggested that Samantha do it herself. So in November of 1982, she did.

Many newspaper, magazine, and TV stories on Andropov focused on his KGB background, his historic suppression of dissidents, and predicted new threats to the West. *Time* magazine published a cover story on Andropov in November 1982, which Smith and her mother read together.

Reagan was president. American and Soviet leaders had not met in years. The Cold War was at its peak. Imagine the surprise when, on April 26, 1983, Samantha received a letter from Andropov, acknowledging her letter from the previous November and inviting her and her family to visit the Soviet Union.

Overnight, Samantha became the most famous little girl in the world. Her letter was published in *Pravda*. On July 7, 1983, the Smith family left for Moscow. During the Cold War, many in the Soviet Union had a negative image of all Americans, so the sight of Samantha playing and swimming with Soviet kids for two weeks humanized Americans. Foreign media followed the family's every move. She never did meet Andropov, but the trip thawed the relationship between the two countries.

For two years afterward, Samantha was an unofficial goodwill ambassador, traveling around the country and to other countries, such as Japan. Then, on August 25, 1985, when Samantha was thirteen, on a return trip from London with her father, their small commercial plane crashed at Auburn-Lewiston Municipal Airport, killing all eight aboard.

Samantha Smith (center, with shoulder bag) attending the Artek Young Pioneer camp in the Soviet Union.

"Everyone in the Soviet Union who has known Samantha Smith will forever remember the image of the American girl who, like millions of Soviet young men and women, dreamt about peace, and about friendship between the peoples of the United States and the Soviet Union."

—*Mikhail Gorbachev*

Samantha's mother, Jane Smith, founded the Samantha Smith Foundation to promote student exchanges between the Soviet Union and the United States. It became dormant in the mid-1990s and dissolved in 2014. A monument was erected in Samantha's honor in Moscow; the Soviet Union issued a stamp in her honor; a Soviet astronomer named an asteroid for her; a Danish composer wrote a concert in her memory; and a diamond from Siberia, a mountain in the former USSR, flowers, and a ship have all been named for her.

Samantha was also posthumously awarded the Peace Abbey Courage of Conscience Award in 2008. American schools have been named for her and several TV shows have included plot lines based on her story.

In Maine, the first Monday of June is Samantha Smith Day. Outside the Maine State Museum in Augusta stands a bronze statue depicting the girl releasing a dove while a bear cub, symbolizing Russia, sits near her feet. Inside the museum, an exhibit honoring her memory includes photographs and artifacts from her Russian trip.

John Ford

JOHN FORD HAS BEEN CALLED "THE GREAT AMERICAN DIRECTOR" AND HIS RECORD of four Academy Awards for Best Director is still unbroken. Although he is best remembered for his westerns, all the awards were for non-Western dramas.

FORDS BEST DIRECTOR ACADEMY AWARDS

The Informer, 1936
The Grapes of Wrath, 1941,
How Green Was My Valley, 1942
The Quiet Man, 1953

He also won two Best Director Oscars for his U.S. Navy documentaries, *The Battle of Midway* in 1942, and *December 7th* in 1943, giving him the unprecedented record of winning back-to-back Best Director Academy Awards in two categories.

Ford was born John Martin "Jack" Feeney in Cape Elizabeth on February 1, in 1894. His parents had emigrated from Ireland and had eleven children, although only six survived to adulthood. Ford would say his name was Sean Aloysius O'Feeney, or O'Fearna. His parents called him Sean. Since they were from Ireland's west coast, where Gaelic is still prevalent, it is likely he was actually christened Sean Aloysius O'Fearna and that his fluency in Gaelic was learned at home.

Ford followed his older brother Francis to Hollywood in 1914. Francis, who was acting and directing, had changed his name to Ford for professional reasons, so John did the same, calling himself Jack Ford. When he arrived in Hollywood, he worked as an actor, a stuntman, and did a lot of production jobs, often for his brother, but within just a few years, he was directing. His first major grossing picture was a 1924 historical epic, *The Iron Horse,* about the first transcontinental railroad. It ran over time and budget, employed 5,000 extras, many thousands of animals, and required the construction of two towns.

When talkies came in, Ford was one of the pioneers, shooting the first song ever filmed for a movie in Fox's 1928 *Mother Machree.* It was also John Wayne's first

film—he was an extra—and the start of a long productive collaboration for both, as well as a lifelong friendship. In 1928, Ford made five features. After that, up until World War II, he made two or three films a year.

Ford was noted for his efficiency and economy of style. Director John Milius compared Ford's style to the Japanese "conservation of line." Ford could create art with commercial appeal and usually do it quickly and under budget. One of the only times Ford commented on his style, he called it "invisible technique," or an attempt to make viewers forget they were watching a movie. He usually kept the cameras around eye level, and hardly moved them. He told young directors to "make sure you can see their eyes."

"Ford could control the movement of the sky in Monument Valley.
The rest of us have to use sound stages."

—Howard Hawks

Many revered directors considered Ford at least one of the best, if not the absolute best. Orson Welles reportedly watched Ford's 1939 *Stagecoach* forty times before he began filming *Citizen Kane*.

> **"I like the old masters, by which I mean John Ford, John Ford, and John Ford."**
>
> —*Orson Welles*

Ingmar Bergman called him the greatest director who ever lived. His other outspoken fans included Martin Scorsese, Clint Eastwood, Sergio Leone, Frank Capra, Howard Hawks, Jean Luc-Godard, Alfred Hitchcock, and Federico Fellini. Steven Spielberg and George Lucas are also big fans.

> **"It can be said that all recent American cinema derives from John Ford's *The Searchers*."**
>
> — *Film critic Stuart Byron*

Ford was awarded a star on the Hollywood Walk of Fame in 1960 and a Presidential Medal of Freedom from Richard Nixon in 1973. He died on August 31, 1973, at age 79, in Palm Desert, California, after a long life of heavy smoking and drinking. He had married Mary McBride in 1920 and they stayed married despite his many affairs. She died the same year. They had two children.

In the 1930s, Ford joined the U.S. Naval Reserve and when World War II came along, he made a few war movies and documentaries. The film he re-enacted at Pearl Harbor the day after the attack is often used as if it was newsreel footage.

For his service and his film work, he received the following military honors: Legion of Merit, Purple Heart, Naval Reserve Medal, American Defense Service Medal, American Campaign Medal, Asiatic-Pacific Campaign Medal with three campaign stars, European-African Middle Eastern Campaign Medal with campaign star, World War II Victory Medal, Navy Occupation Medal, National Defense Service Medal, Korean Service Medal, and the United Nations Korea Medal. The title of honorable admiral was conferred on him for his work, and his tombstone reads "Admiral John Ford."

www.ingramcontent.com/pod-product-compliance
Lightning Source LLC
Chambersburg PA
CBHW060755150426
42811CB00058B/1418

9781608936311